PLANES and PILOT

German Jets
of World War II

Dominique Breffort
Drawings André Jouineau
Translated from the French by Alan McKay

HISTOIRE & COLLECTIONS

MESSERSCHMITT ME 262 SCHWALBE

Although chronologically speaking the Messerschmitt 262 was not the first jet-powered aircraft in the history of flying it was nonetheless the first jet plane to be mass produced and used intensively in operations and with undeniable success during the last year of the conflict.

It could have been even more successful if its strategic use hadn't been, at the beginning at least, subject to the illogical decisions of Hitler himself who saw the plane as a fast bomber rather instead of an air superiority fighter, a kind of fighter for which the Allies didn't yet have an counterpart - far from it.

The first turbojet trials in Germany took place in September 1937 at the University of Gottingen under the leadership of Hans Joachim Pabst von Ohain. He took out a patent in 1936 for a jet engine of his own design and was quickly taken on by the Heinkel firm in Rostock. Creating a truly independent cell inside this company with his mechanic Max Hahn, von Ohain made his first engine, the HeS 1, which worked on the bench as early as 1937 and was quickly followed by a single flow engine with liquid fuel, the HeS 3B rated at 1 100 lbf (550 kgp) thrust. This engine was installed into a plane specially designed for it, the Heinkel He 178, the first jet propelled machine to be designed in Germany and which made its maiden flight on 27 August 1939.

Exactly one year before that date, at the end of the summer of 1938, the RLM, or Reichsluftfahrtministerium, the German Air Ministry, had set up a study group under the leadership of the engineers Hans Much and Helmut Schelp, with the job of developing the engines ("TL"). This group was doubled up by another whose task was to do research on a machine capable of being fitted with this new type of engine, among whom was Hans Antz, who encouraged Wilhelm "Willy" Messerschmitt to design an airframe which could be equipped with a gas turbine or rockets.

After various meetings, Messerschmitt started working on "Projekt 1065", which was presented in October 1938 to the Technische Amt of the RLM (the Technical Service of the German Air Ministry) which ordered it officially. It was a twin-engined plane, a layout which was preferred because the jet engine chosen to equip it, the rather simply designed BMW P. 3320 with an axial compressor, close to von Ohain's, didn't produce enough thrust.[1] The engines were attached to the main spar and sunk into the wings.

Messerschmitt envisaged a range of 30 minutes, whereas the armament was deliberately limited in order to save weight. The undercarriage was conventional with a retractable tail wheel, and the tail was triangular with the horizontal stabilisers placed high up.

As a result of BMW announcing that its future engines performed better and would finally be wider, Messerschmitt sent the RLM a revised project. It was 26 ft 3 in (8.30 m) long, 6 ½ ft (2.80 m) high, with a 29 ½ ft (9.40 m) wing span for an all-up weight of 8 818 lb (4 300 kg); the "new" P. 1065

The V3 prototype was the first to fly using its own jet engines on 18 July 1942.

The V2 was the third prototype to fly on 1 October 1942. The presence of a tail wheel hindered take off as the elevators were inoperable because of the plane's angle of attack; the pilot had to break during the take off run to get the tail into the air…

was to be capable of reaching 560 mph (900 kph), with its two engines rated at 1 322 lbf (600 kg) each.

Since the RLM authorised the research to be continued, it also financed the building of a wooden scale 1 model of the new machine which it was able to examine in January 1940. Twenty trial P. 1065s were officially ordered the following month, on which it was decided to install BMW P3302s. At the same time, the new plane's standard equipment was decided on (pressurised cockpit, ejector seat, etc.) and the modifications were announced in a report drawn up by the Messerschmitt research group boss, Woldemar Voigt, on 21 March. The fuselage had an almost triangular cross section, with a teardrop canopy and the outside part of the wings were swept back in order to compensate for moving the centre of gravity. The position of the engines, sunk into the wings, wasn't changed, neither were the tail wheel, the original tail fin and the position of the armament at the front of the fuselage.

At the time however, no engine capable of powering these prototypes was available. Indeed, apart from Heinkel (three prototypes of his He 280 had been ordered in March), only BMW and Junkers had shown any interest in the subject and each proposed a model of engine specific to the P.1065, the only official requirement being a maximum unit thrust of 1 540 lbf (700 kgp). After giving up on a first model, BMW concentrated on the simple axial flow P.3302 (officially designated 109-003A), which was tried out in August 1940 but initially was only rated at 330 lbf (150 kgp); this thrust was increased to 990 lbf (450 kgp) after a lot of modifications had been made.

The situation was even less brilliant at Junkers where although the 109-004 (or "T1") engine had indeed worked on the bench in November 1940, developing it was taking even more time, with the first trials – on a Bf 110 – only starting in March 1942…

As BMW had announced that its modified engine would have a wider diameter, Messerschmitt had to modify his project, especially as the engines could no longer be partly sunk into the wings. On 15 May 1940, a simpler, revised P.1065 project was therefore submitted to the RLM, taking into account all the modifications announced in W. Voigt's report a few days earlier. Finally on 1 November, a "Type III" P.1065 was presented; it was the same as the previous two except for the position of the engines which were now attached under the wings, which made building the plane and servicing the engines easier. The project was given the official go-ahead on 19 December 1940 in the form of an order for a further twenty trial machines, together with fifteen pre-production models. The new plane was officially designated Me 262 in February 1941 and nicknamed "Schwalbe" (swallow).

As building the prototypes had begun at the Messerschmitt Augsburg factory in April 1940, less than a year later, on 8 April 1941, the first was

Ordered by the RLM at the same time as the Me 262, the Heinkel He 280 was the first jet fighter in the history of flying to take to the air, on 30 March 1941, when Fritz Schäfer took the V2 up for its first flight. In the end they only built eight examples (including three prototypes) of this plane, equipped with tricycle undercarriage, and from the outset with an ejector seat.

ready, but the engines needed for it to fly were not; so much so that a meeting took place to determine what means of propulsion was to be used for this inaugural flight. After the Walter rockets had been discarded, it was finally decided to use a conventional engine… with pistons and a propeller! A Junkers Jumo 210G [2] rated at 700 bhp and driving a two-blade propeller was therefore installed in the nose, which was specially redesigned for the occasion. So it was in this rather unconventional configuration that the first prototype, the Me 262 V1 (PC+UA), made its first flight on 18 April 1941, with Flugkapitän Fritz Wendel, Messerschmitt's chief test pilot, at the controls. A few days later on 30 March, Heinkel flew its He 280, equipped with two jet engines rated at 1 100 lbf (500 kg) each. With the V1 carrying out seven other test flights before the end of July during which, even though obviously underpowered, it managed to reach 337.5 mph (540 kph) in a dive, the RLM changed its initial order on 25 July 1941 and Messerschmitt now had to build five prototypes and twenty pre-production series machines.

Almost at the same time, the first pair of BMW 109-003A jet engines were finally available and were fitted to the Me 262 V1 which carried out

---

1. A jet engine using a similar technique was also developed in Great Britain by Frank Whittle who was considered along with von Ohain, as the inventor of the jet engine, for which he took out patents as early as 1930. The similarities between the research carried out by the two engineers caused the German to be suspected of plagiarism, which was finally refuted. The first machine to fly powered by an engine designed by Frank Whittle, the Gloster E28/39, made its first flight on 15 May 1941.
2. This inverted V-12 was installed in all Messerschmitt Bf 109s (versions A to D) and Bf 110 (A and B), as well as in the Junkers Ju 87A.

ground tests in this configuration for several months before finally taking to the air on 25 March 1942. The piston engine already installed was retained and as it happened this turned out to be very useful because the machine had hardly got airborne when both engines went out one after the other and Wendel needed all his flying skills to bring the plane back to earth safely…

The cause of this incident was very quickly found: vibrations had broken some of the fan blades causing the engines to go out, a breakdown which was to occur often enough all throughout the plane's career. The trials were suspended while waiting for new engines. On 29 May, the RLM reduced its order to five prototypes and fifteen pre-production machines, the latter to be built only at the end of the trials, if these were conclusive.

A pre-production series of Junkers 109-004A-0 engines, which were more reliable and more powerful (1 873 lb s.t./850 kg) than the BMWs, were finally available at the beginning of the summer of 1942 and were fitted onto the third prototype (V3, PC+UC) which had come off the production line on 1 June. Fitting these new engines had meant modifying the nacelles because they were longer and wider, and the tail was enlarged in order to improve lateral stability.

The V3 was sent to the airfield at Lechfeld, near Augsburg, which was unusual in that it had a concrete runway and a lot of empty space.[3]

Taxiing trials immediately revealed weaknesses in the elevators because of the nose-up attitude caused by the tail wheel. To get round this, a take-off technique was found by trial and error, consisting of forcing the aircraft's nose down by breaking during the take off run at a particular spot on the runway marked out with paint. Once the machine was in this position, the elevators recovered all their effectiveness.

The Me 262 V3 took to the air for the first time using its own jet engines on 18 July 1942 and carried out two other fifteen-minute flights without any particular incident. As six further flights were made while they were at it, flown by test pilots from Messerschmitt, it was decided to allow a pilot from the Luftwaffe's test unit, the Erprobungsstelle at Rechlin, Heinrich Beauvais, to take it up. On 11 August, after trying to get the V3 off the ground twice, he went off the runway during the third attempt and crashed after somersaulting… Although extensively damaged, the prototype was considered reparable.

A few weeks after this accident, it was the turn of a third prototype, Me 262 V2 (PC+UB) also equipped with Jumo 109004A-0s, to take to the air,

flown by Fritz Wendel. As a matter of interest, the day after this inaugural flight, there was another one: that of the Bell XP-59, the first jet plane built in the USA.

The RLM up till now had only shown lukewarm interest in the programme but now it got more involved, ordering a further five prototypes and ten pre-production machines (V11 to V20) the next day from Messerschmitt, but these were to have tricycle undercarriage and different armament. This order was followed by another on 2 October for thirty pre-production machines, to be delivered before the end of 1943, a target the aircraft builder considered to be impossible to reach, though this didn't prevent the authorities from envisaging monthly production figures of twenty machines from 1944 onwards…

Nonetheless Messerschmitt carried on with the trials with the V1 itself being fitted with Jumo 004 engines at the beginning of March 1943; its propeller-driven engine was removed; an extra prototype, Me 262 V4, was delivered to Lechfeld the following month and flight tested by the "boss" of the German fighters, Generalleutnant Adolf Galland in person. After making some remarks about the range of the aircraft, thought to be insufficient, he said he was enthusiastic about the new jet fighter. After he wrote to the Luftwaffe's Chief Inspector, Generalfeldmarschall Erhard Milch, to vaunt the new fighter's virtues. It would, if produced in sufficient numbers, give Germany a decisive advantage over the Allies. He once again told Göring about his excellent impressions the following May during an official interview, asking for all Luftwaffe fighters to be jets except for the Fw 190!

TECHNICAL SPECIFICATIONS Me 262A-1a

Type
Single-seat jet fighter

Powerplant
Two Junkers Jumo 004B turbojets each rated at 1 980 lbf (900 kgp)

Dimensions
Wingspan: 41 ft 6 in (12.65 m)
Wing area: 233.576 sq ft (21.70 m²)
Length: 34 ft 9 in (10.60 m)
Height: 12 ft 6 in (3.85 m)
Weight (Empty): 8 800 lb (4 000 kg)
Take-off weight (loaded): 15 334 lb (6 970 kg)

Performances
Max. Speed: 500 mph (800 kph) at sea

level; 544 mph (870 kph) at 19 700 ft (6 000 m); 528 mph (845 kph) at 29 500 ft (9 000 m)

Operational ceiling: 37 400 ft (11 400 m)

Range: 187-220 mph (300-350 km) at sea level; 325-375 mph (520-600 km) at 19 700 ft (6 000 m);406-437 mph (650-700 km) at 29 500 ft (9 000 m)

Rate of climb: 19 700 ft (6 000 m) in 7 minutes; 29 500 ft (9 000 m) in 14 minutes

Take-off run: 1 006 yards (920 m)

Landing speed: 114 mph (182 kph)

Armament
Four 30-mm 80 or 100-round MK 108 cannon

---

3. The official code name of the Me 262 was "Silber" (silver) and the "Silber Bases" like Lechfeld or Leipheim were specially prepared to receive the jet: concrete runway, stocks of spare parts, JE fuel tanks and specially trained mechanics.

The Reichsmarschall politely but firmly refused but in June 1943 he did ratify the decision to launch mass production of the Me 262, this being planned (sub-contractors, delays, etc.) within the framework of "Program 223". Production rate was fixed at 60 aircraft per month, a figure to be reached the following year, in May 1944. This schedule wasn't to Willy Messerschmitt's liking, quite unconvinced as he was by the RLM deciding on the course of action without consulting him. In this rather tense atmosphere, Messerschmitt decided to continue with the trials as quickly as possible. The V5, fitted with fixed tricycle undercarriage took to the air on 6 June 1943 but the behaviour of this prototype turned out to be poor, mainly because the forward undercarriage leg caused so much drag, that take off rockets had to be fitted to help the plane.

The Me 262 V6, the first pre-production series machine[4] fitted with retractable undercarriage and new, more powerful (rated at 1 984 lbf/900 kg each) Jumo 004B-1 engines, meaning the nacelles had to be redesigned, took off on its maiden flight in November 1943, quickly followed by the V7, the first machine with the definitive, pressurised cockpit.

At the end of 1943 several new examples were available, the V8 (the first armed example), the V10 (used for rudder trials) and especially the V9 ("HG" for *Hochgeschwindigkeit* – high speed), finished in January 1944 and equipped with a faired, lower canopy to be used as a high speed record plane; it reached the speed of 1 004 kph in a shallow dive on 6 June 1944, a record which went by unnoticed because of the date!

"Even a child can see it's a fighter not a bomber!"

However, a completely unexpected event was to compromise the career of the Me 262, at the very time when mass production had only just started[5].

Convinced ever since autumn 1943 that the first hours after an Allied landing on the European coast would be decisive and that a few hundred fast bombers attacking the beaches would pin the enemy down and give the Panzer units time to reach the front, Hitler saw the Messerschmitt 262, at the time right in the middle of its development, as the miracle weapon which would be able to turn the situation around in the event of an invasion.

On 2 November 1943, Hermann Göring and Erhard Milch went to Augsburg where the Reichsmarschall told Willy Messerschmitt about the Führer's idea and asked the designer if the Me 262 could carry bombs. The latter answered that such a configuration had been thought of from the outset and at the cost of modifications taking only a few weeks' time, the twin-engined plane could carry a 1 100 lb (500-kg) or two 550-lb (250-kg) bombs. On 26 November at Intersburg, two Schwalbes (prototypes V4 and V7) were officially presented to the Führer himself together with the most modern German machines being developed at the time. Hitler repeated his question to Willy Messerschmitt who answered without hesi-

tating "it can carry a one-thousand kilo bomb without any difficulty."

Whereupon the dictator, who was satisfied, replied *"This is just the plane I've been asking for years but nobody was capable of designing it."*

On 20 December during a staff meeting he repeated what his strategy would be in the event of an Allied landing, now taking into account the use of the Me 262: *"It is capable of pinning down the enemy on the beaches for six to eight hours."*

On 23 May 1944, Göring, Milch, Galland (Fighters' CO), Albert Speer (the Production Minister), took part in a meeting at Bechtesgaden, Hitler's HQ, together with a lot of Luftwaffe bigwigs. As soon as the subject of the Me 262 was brought up, Hitler immediately asked *"How many examples capable of carrying bombs have been made?"* Milch having answered none, after a few moments of silence, the dictator broke out into a furious rage. *"All that I asked for was a 250-kg bomb! Doesn't anybody take any notice of my orders?"* Then after the features of the plane were explained to him, he carried on: *"There's no need for machine guns and it's so fast that it is invulnerable and doesn't need any armour."* Among this audience petrified by such fury, only Göring dared to declare: *"But my Führer, even a little child can see that it's a fighter not a bomber!"*

There was no changing his mind and four days later on the 27th, the Reichsmarschall sent a telegram to Milch: *"The Führer has ordered the Me 262 to be used as a fast bomber only. As from now and unless otherwise ordered, this machine must no longer be considered as a fighter."* Even its name was changed, the bomber version being called the Sturmvogel (storm-petrel).

To satisfy the Hitler's demands, Me 262 V10 VI+AE, WNr 130005, the last prototype, was hastily equipped with two bomb racks fitted behind the nose wheel well, but this prototype was quickly destroyed during trials, with its pilot managing to bale out… The bomber version had its armour reduced and its armament reduced to two 20-mm cannon, and two fuel tanks were installed in the fuselage. Moreover downwards visibility was greatly restricted and threatened to jeopardise bombing missions; so much so that for a while it was envisaged to add an aperture in the cockpit floor. Bombing was done by means of Zeiss TSA 2A sights and the bombs were fitted to ETC 501 then 503 pylons which were eventually given fairings called *Wikingerschiff* (Viking ship) because of their shape which was designed to prevent vibrations encountered on the standard models. On 22 July 1944, a conference of the Jägerstab – the fighters' recently created general staff – was held during which

---

4. In order to speed up the trials before mass production it was decided to use the pre-production series machines or Me 262A-0s as prototypes, which received a "V" (for Versuchmuster) code.
5. In February 1944, 23 pre-production series Me 262A-0s had been built by Messerschmitt but not all of them had their engines. Delivery of these machines to the Luftwaffe started the following April, 8 being sent to the Erprobungsstelle at Rechlin for trials and 15 to the Erprobungskommando 262 based at Lechfeld.

Me 262A-1a «White 4» belonging to the Erprobungskommando 262. The white individual number on the front of the fuselage and the thin yellow line round the rear were the characteristic markings of this unit. The nose wheel was equipped with a scissors damper on the early models, and was then replaced by an internal shock absorber, as here. (USAF Museum)

the Me 262-production schedule was set out with 500 examples to be supplied to the Luftwaffe for the month of December 1944 alone. In fact the reality of the situation was quite different for between July and the end of the same year, only 513 Schwalbe were delivered. The Luftwaffe itself got involved in the test programme from June 1944 on, when several Me 262s were delivered to the Erprobungsstelle (E-Stelle, test centre) at Rechlin. The following month, the number of these machines rose to thirteen and the unit had flown 800 flying hours by September of the same year. The trials at the E-Stelle carried on till the beginning of 1945, with some aircraft being given the V codes of earlier, damaged machines, and in all thirty-five production series examples were supplied for all sorts of trials.

Me 262 Units

The Erprobungskommando 262

On 9 September 1943, the General der Jagdflieger asked for an experimental unit to be created and equipped with jet fighters. Erprobungskommando 262 was therefore formed at Lechfeld, an airfield situated south of Augsburg where the Messerschmitt factory was located. Originally twenty pilots made up this EKdo 262, which was put under the command of Hauptmann Werner Thierfelder, a former Bf 110 pilot who had been Gruppenkommandeur of the III./ZG 26.

The first three student pilots arrived in January 1944 at Lechfeld where only one Me 262 (the V5) was available… At the end of April 1944, the unit was supplied with two other prototypes, among which the V8, the first to have been armed, as well as two pre-production series machines. The following month, a dozen pilots were transferred to Lechfeld, coming from the 8. And 9./ZG 26, units previously commanded by Thierfelder and equipped with Messerschmitt 410s. Apart from the EKdo 262's CO's wish to have men he knew with him, this choice was explained by the fact that it was thought that a pilot used to flying twin-engined aircraft, even a propeller-driven ones, would be able to master the Me 262 quicker as it too was twin-engined.

In reality this turned out to be quite wrong and the pilots had a lot of trouble getting used to the jet, not only because of its tricycle undercarriage – a very rare configuration at the time for a Luftwaffe plane – but also because it had performances which up until then the pilots had never dealt with – the Me 262 had a 40% higher top speed than the

Me 410! Losses started piling up, the first being on 19 May 1944 when *Uffizier* Kurt Flachs was killed aboard V7 during a simple training flight.

On 25 May, as we have seen, Hitler who was furious that his orders to change the Me 262 into a fast bomber hadn't been obeyed, put EKdo 262 under the authority of the *General der Kampfflieger* (the Bombers CO). Some of the students who hadn't finished their conversion had therefore to go back to their old unit, but Thierfelder surreptitiously decided on his own initiative to pursue the fighter training with eight pilots and the few machines which were still available. Sadly, he died in circumstances that are still unclear during a reconnaissance flight on 18 July 1944 and was replaced by *Hauptmann* Horst Geyer at the head of EKdo 262.

On the 26th of the same month, the unit scored its first kill when *Leutnant* Alfred Schreiber shot down a Mosquito in the Munich region, with the British machine having to make an emergency landing in Italy. Another kill, not officially confirmed, was claimed a week later. The EKdo 262's first "real" kill, and therefore the first ever by a jet, took place on 8 August 1944, when an Me 262 flown by *Leutnant* Joachim Weber, shot down a Mosquito PR XVI from No 540 Squadron in the Munich area. Exactly a week later, the unit scored its one and only USAAF B-17 bomber.

Against Hitler's wishes, Galland reinforced the EKdo 262 by increasing its strength to 40 aircraft in two Staffeln, the first commanded by *Oberleutnant* Muller and the second by *Oberleutnant* Bley. Both units were sent to Rechlin-Lärz, their transfer being complete on 21 August. The first combat sortie took place on 10 September but only two kills were scored (on 14 and 18 September). A small detachment of the EKdo 262, under *Oberleutnant* Wegmann (and therefore called "Kommando Wegmann") was sent to Erfurt but in fact, most of this unit's kills scored before it was disbanded were obtained by pilots who had remained at Lechfeld. When he changed his mind about using the Me 262 only as a fast bomber, Hitler agreed that the plane be used only in the fighter version… At the end of September, when the EKdo 262 had twelve machines and seventeen pilots, Galland reorganised the units equipped with Schwalbe: the Rechlin and Erfurt detachments, as well as the one based at Lechfeld, were sent to Achmer and Hesepe to constitute an Einsatzkommando (special detachment) and the EKdo 262 Stab was absorbed into the Ergänzjagdgeschwader 2 (EJG2/ operational training group 2) based at Lechfeld.

The Einsatzkommando Schenk

As a result of Hitler's order to use the Me 262 only as a bomber, the Kampfgeschwader 51 "Eidelweiss" was chosen to be become the first operational unit to convert to this type. On 23 May 1944, the Stab and the 8. Gruppe left France where they had been stationed with their Me 410s and reached the test base at Lechfeld. The Me 262s were urgently transformed into bombers (the A-2a version of which Messerschmitt produced 28 examples in June 1944 alone), this conversion consisting mainly of increasing the plane's range with two extra fuel tanks, one 66-gallon (250-litre) tank under the pilot's seat and a 158-gallon (600-litre) one at the rear of the fuselage. Apart from the fact that this modification changed the centre of gravity when fully loaded, and although the two upper cannon and part of the armour were removed, the plane was heavier than planned, which meant reinforcing the landing gear.

The 3./KG 51, commanded by *Major* Schenk, was the first to get the planes, in fact those from the EKdo 262 hastily modified, with the pilot conversion programme being speeded up after the Allied landings in Normandy on 6 June 1944. A dozen pilots very quickly made up the Einsatzkommando Schenk, named after their CO, and got nine Me 262s with which they were sent to France on 20 July. Worried about not wasting a single valued "*Blitzbombern*" (lightning bombers) or seeing them falling into enemy hands, the staff ordered them not to fly below 13 120 ft (4 000 m) and more than 466 mph (750 kph) so the bombers impact was reduced to nothing, so much so that the Allies were not even aware of their incursions which went by quite unnoticed…

Moreover because of the advancing Allies, the Kommando Schenk's Me 262s had to fall back quickly, settling first at Creil, then at Juvincourt from where they carried out several missions, especially against targets situated to the northwest of Paris or in the region of Melun, after being reinforced by five – out of the nine which left Germany – Schwalbes.

After moving off again to Chièvres, near Brussels on 28 August, the unit encountered enemy fighters for the first time, one of its pilots being forced to make a belly landing in order to escape a USAAF P-47 which was chasing it…

On 5 September, the Kommando Schenk was disbanded and incorporated into the 3./JG 51 which quickly joined the I./JG 51 based at Rheine. Schenk remained reasonably autonomous for a few weeks after being disbanded by using the Kommando Edelweiss, equipped with… two machines, used mainly for various tests, particularly for the sights and bombing systems.

The Ergänzjagdgeschwader 2 (EJG 2)

After Galland's reorganisation, EKdo 262 became the III./EJG 2 at the end of September 1944 and was given the job of training Schwalbe pilots. Led by *Hauptmann* Horst Geyer, it was meant to consist of 122 planes (four times more than a normal *Gruppe*). In point of fact this figure was never reached since in the month following its creation, it numbered a dozen instructors and about seventy pupils but only two Me 262s! Nonetheless the situation got better rapidly since finally it had some twenty planes (including two two-seaters), and the number of instructors and pupils went up too.

On 1 December 1944, the III./EJG 2 was reorganised for the first time: the 9. Staffel was based at Landsberg with propeller aircraft for training; the 10. stayed at Lechfeld with the Stab and the 11. was sent to Unterschlauerbach, near Nuremberg. In fact this airfield with its grass strips quickly turned out to be unsuitable for the Me 262s, with the Staffel having only a few old machines supplied by the 10. and no two-seaters.

Converting pilots to the Schwalbe started by twenty hours' training aboard single-engined planes (Bf 109G or Ks, Fw 190S two-seaters) for the former twin engined bomber pilots, before going on to a period of getting used to the Me 262, especially to handling the delicate

Captured by the American 5th Armored Division on the airfield at Stendal on 15 April, this " Yellow 8" (WNr 112385) from the 3./JG 7 "Nowotny" had its left engine damaged by its own flak a few days earlier. It is camouflaged with large stripes of RLM 81 and 82 on the fuselage and wings, and the red and blue stripe attributed to this group. (US National Archives)

Opposite.
Ready for take-off for Me 262A-1a "Green 5" from the Stab of the JG 7 "Nowotny" at Brandenburg-Briest. In this unit, the planes had their number painted in small figures under the insignia in front of the windshield.

throttles. Then the pupils were sent to the 9./EJG 2 which was equipped with twin-engined Bf 110s, Siebel 204s or Fw 54s, before taking to a jet for a series of ground manoeuvres and then finally carrying out their first solo flight, followed by patrol flying and firing practice. In fact this theoretical training was very rarely completed as it was constantly being modified to fit the circumstances (the evolution of the fighting in the air, the chronic lack of fuel, etc.) or the weather which restricted all activity considerably, if it didn't ground the aircraft altogether for days even weeks on end. Although the EJG 2's activity was peppered with incidents and even accidents some of them fatal, the unit did score several kills, for example a P-38 shot down on 5 February 1945, two P-51s and two B-17s the following month, kills obtained by *Hauptmann* Wilhelm Steinmann alone, with *Oberst* Walter Dahl claming two other kills in March.

On 1 January 1945, *Major* Heinz Bär, until then the JG 3 *Kommodore* replaced Geyer as the III./EJG 2's CO and obtained almost a third of the kills scored by the unit before the end of the war! [6]

The Kommando Nowotny

As we saw above, some pilots and machines (thirty or so) from EKdo 262, based at Achmer and Hesepe hadn't been incorporated into the III./ EJG 262 when this was set up. They were used with other elements [7] to form a new unit, created specially by Adolf Galland and commanded by the Luftwaffe's ace of aces on the Eastern Front (255 kills), *Major* Walter Nowotny and therefore called Kommando Nowotny. At first this group was the victim of a number of accidents, so much so that after barely a month's existence, it only had four Me 262s left still

in flying condition… Then its situation improved dramatically because, against Hitler's orders, out of the 52 fighters of this type delivered to the Luftwaffe, all but one were assigned to this detachment!

Although it wasn't totally operational, the Kommando Nowotny made its first combat sorties on 7 October from its airfields at Hesepe and Achmer. Nonetheless after several machines were shot down by marauding Allied fighters using a tactic which was soon to become widespread [8], it was decided to assign some Fw 190Ds from 9. and 10./JG 54, Nowotny's former group, to protect the Schwalbe's bases. This solution turned out to be very costly because on only 12 October, the 9./JG 54 lost six of its Doras…

The following day, after two Me 262s were lost in an accident, the planes were grounded for two weeks, with operations only resuming on 28 October. After that the accidents carried on occurring just as did the kills, with four jets being lost on 7 November alone. Worse still, the following day it was the turn of Major Nowotny himself to be killed, in circumstances which remain unclear even today (probably an engine breakdown); this occurred near Hesepe airfield in front of several witnesses including Adolf Galland himself, who was there because he happened to be on an inspection tour the day before… Just before he disappeared, Nowotny, the third pilot in the unit to be shot down on 8 November, had just scored his third kill aboard an Me 262.

In the end the Kommando Nowotny did not survive the death of its leader. Although he was replaced by *Oberleutnant* Eder, the last combat mission took place on 17 November when most of the pilots had been sent to Lechfeld to be re-equipped. Having obtained 18 confirmed kills for the loss of 26 lost or damaged Me 262s [9], the Kommando Nowotny was in turn used to train a new unit, Jagdgeschwader 7.

Below.
This Schwalbe (WNr 500071 – "White 3") from 9./JG 7 flown by Fähnrich Hans-Guido Mutke was forced to land at Zurich, Switzerland when it ran out of fuel after having tried to intercept a formation of B-26s in the south of Germany, on 25 April 1945.

---

6. In detail: one P-51D on 13 March, a B-24D on the 21st, a B-24D and a Mustang on the 24th, two B-26s on 9 April, two P-47s on the 18th and finally two P-51s on 19 April. Because of the Allies' inexorable advance into Germany, the Lechfeld base had to be evacuated on 23 April 1945 and its occupants sent to Munich-Reim. From there the pupils who had been already trained, as well as their instructors, joined JG 7 which was based in Prague, and a small group of pilots including Bär, remained in Munich where they were incorporated into JV 44.

7. Apart from the Einsatzkommando, the Stab of the III./ZG 26 and the EKdo 262, the Kommando Nowotny comprised three Staffeln, the 1. And 2. formed from the 9. and 8./ZG respectively, and the 3., started from scratch.

8. As with the other German jets (Me 163, AR 234 and Heinkel 162), the Allies noticed that the Schwalbes were particularly vulnerable when flying slowly and especially when landing. So the technique consisted of "rat catching" – keeping patrols of fighters (Mustangs, Thunderbolts, Tempests, etc.) on permanent alert which took off as soon as radar detected Me 262s approaching their home bases. Flying at 3 000 m in the neighbourhood of the airfields, the fighters only had to pick off the almost defenceless Schwalbes as they landed. The Germans reacted by getting the jets to approach their bases at top speed and low altitude and then only slow down as soon as they were within the defensive circle formed by the flak. The British who had shot down eight Me 262s thus lost seven Tempests during the same period.

9. The Kommando Nowotny's first two losses in combat were on 10 October 1944, one week after the jet was declared operational. The Schwalbes were shot down by P-51 Mustangs escorting bombers that they were attacking. As for the accidents caused by technical problems, one third was due to undercarriage defects, another third due to the power plant (the turbo-compressor blades breaking, fires, etc.) and 10% due to the engine causing vibrations which broke the tail unit.

The JG 7 "Nowotny"

The Jagdgeschwader 7 was the main and largest Me 262 user and it had more pilots and planes than any other unit of its type during its seven months' existence. It numbered among its pilots the highest number of Schwalbe Experten (Aces). It is estimated that its two groups (Stab and III.) with, on average, forty or so Me 262s, accounted for almost five hundred kills, of which three hundred were heavy bombers, or more than 75% of the kills the Schwalbe scored during its short career of less than ten months.

Formed in August 1944 from the remnants of Kampfgeschwader 1 (KG 1), it was originally supposed to have comprised two Fw 190 Gruppen, quickly replaced by Messerschmitt Bf 109G-14s. As this turned out not to be possible because there weren't any planes, it was decided at the end of autumn 1944 to increase its strength to three Gruppen and to give it a certain number of Me 262s. Commanded by the *Geschwaderkommodore, Oberstleutnant* Johannes "Macki" Steinhoff, the new JG 7 trained at first at Brandenburg-Briest, then was assembled at Lechfeld in Bavaria during the second week of November. 70% of the group consisted of aces and their desire to have a go at the enemy flying a new fighter was very strong, but their zeal had to be tempered because the planes and the men had to hide for a while to prevent their base from being bombed…

Their first mission finally took place on 28 November and Buchner was the only pilot among the four engaged that day who had managed to get aloft, shooting down a Lockheed F-5 (the recce version of the famous P-38 Lightning).

A lot of the pilots assigned to JG 7 were in fact former Kampfgeschwadern pilots who had a "C" certificate qualifying them to fly a machine weighing more than five tonnes and familiarising them with instrument flying deep into enemy territory. At the time this sort of pilot seemed the most suitable for converting to the Me 262, but this idea was eventually abandoned in March 1945 when it was noticed that the former bomber pilots lacked the boldness and the fervour so necessary to the classic fighter pilot. The JG 7 pilots' conversion was carried out thanks in part to the few Me 262B two-seaters available (about fif-

Above.
Me 262 assembly line at Obertraubling, in the middle of the forest, photographed after the Allies arrived. Damage to the machines was caused by 15th Air Force air raids. *(US National Archives)*

teen in all, modified in the autumn of 1944 by Blohm und Voss in Hamburg), although seven of them were lost in accidents during training…

The III./JG 7 was set up on 19 November 1944 at Lechfeld and Major Erich Hohagen put in charge. It was given the special task of developing new tactics using the Schwalbe but it had trouble reaching operational status, losing ten planes in its first six weeks of existence, mainly through pilot error and for technical reasons. Training slowed down a lot in December because of the very bad weather conditions but when these got better at the end of the month, the first successes started coming in with JG 7 being officially given the task of defending Berlin and its immediate region.

The III./JG 7 was only fully operational in mid-February 1945, a month later than planned, with its three Staffeln all being commanded by aces (respectively *Oberstleutnante* Waldmann, Grünberg and Stehle). At the time, the whole group numbered some fifty or so operational jets.

On 10 March an operation to attack Allied bombers was mounted

A Schwalbe from I./KG 51 abandoned in a sorry state, photographed by American troops near Rhein-Main in March 1945. *(US National Archives)*

Above.
Among the wrecks discovered in the test airfield at Lager-Lechfeld were the engineless V10 and the V9 (in the background), used for high-speed trials and equipped with a lowered canopy. *(US National Archives)*

during which the biggest formation of Me 262 ever assembled was sent aloft. The result of this sortie on the other hand was rather unsatisfactory: out of the 45 planes involved, or all the machines available, (against 1 200 four-engined bombers), only 28 found their targets and only four *Dicke Autos* (the nickname given to the four-engined bombers by the Germans) were shot down by the R4M rockets, a weapon only tried out in combat for the first time the day before. Apart from the huge number of casualties in the pilots' ranks caused by the numerous accidents and the fighting, the JG 7 was also affected by the severe lack of fuel, since the USAAF could attack the "Silber" bases day after day almost with impunity. In spite of this, a number of kills were scored, at least fifty Allied aircraft being shot down during the short period from 18 to 22 March 1945. Even better, on 31 March, 21 heavy bombers were shot down so much so that at the end of the same month, the tally for the JG 7 rose to 108 four-engined bombers and one Mosquito, at a cost of 22 pilots killed and five wounded.

On 1 April 1945, the I./JG 7 was forced to evacuate Kaltenkirchen, its I. Staffel being sent to Brandenburg-Briest; the 2. to Burg and the 3. to Orianenburg. Three days later on 4 April each of these Saffeln was encouraged to operate individually as independent units. At that time the JG 7 had less than 60 jets, fifteen of which were shot down as they took off on 1 April alone…

During the last two weeks of its existence, from mid-April onwards, JG 7's Staffeln were dispersed in Czechoslovakia and in Bavaria in little

Below.
A photograph taken from a colour film made by American troops showing an Me 262A-1a 9K+FH (WNr 111685) from I./KG 51 abandoned on the side of a motorway in the middle of the forest. *(US National Archives)*

groups and without any real command, their final strength at the time of the armistice being some fifteen Me 262s.

The Jagdverband 44

As *General der Jagdflieger* Adolf Galland had been one of the artisans of the so-called "Rebellion of the Fighters" which took place at the end of January 1945 when several senior Luftwaffe officers contested Hermann Göring, the Reichsmarschall reacted in a most spectacular way by demoting Galland and ordering him to the Eastern Front after demoting him to the rank of simple Staffel CO…[10]

Hitler immediately invalidated this sentence when he heard about it and had Galland form a unit the size of a Staffel to show how much better the Me 262 was as a fighter. Having the advantage of being totally independent, Galland's powers were in fact those of a major-general. With the unit having been formed officially on 15 February 1945, Galland chose to set it up at an airfield situated fifty or so km from Berlin, Brandenburg-Briest, used at the time by elements from the JG 77. Designated Jagdverband (fighter unit) 44 [11], the new unit comprising a Stab and three Staffeln (1., 2. and 3.) was created at the beginning of March 1945 and started training immediately.

The JV 44 was made up mainly of *Experten* (Aces) like Barkhorn, Lutzow or Hohagen coming from various horizons, ten of them having been awarded the prestigious Ritterkreuz. It moved to Munich-Riem in order to protect the Messerschmitt factories nearby. As it had carried out only one war mission, Galland increased the number of available machines and pilots to be more effective and fitted a large number of Me 262s with R4M rockets.[12]

Success was not long in coming and on 5 April, a USAAF heavy bomber was shot down and two others damaged. As JV 44's base had been the target of Allied air raids or attacked by marauding fighters, Fw 190 protection was brought in, but this *Papagei Staffel* (parrot squadron, so named after its Doras' red and white striped undersides) was in the end rather unconvincing since the pilots of these piston-engined machines had both to fight against the enemy fighters and avoid their own rather trigger-happy flak gunners.

On 23 April 1944, the JV 44 was reinforced by the III./EJG 2 and the I./KG 51 which settled at Munich, bringing the unit's strength to forty or so Me 262s available and a hundred or so pilots (of which almost half were still training). Galland was shot down on 26 April and replaced by Oberstleutnant Bär who flew one of the very rare Me 262A-1a/U1s armed with six cannon, several times.

When Munich-Riem became unusable because it was overcrowded with all sorts of planes and being bombed continuously, JV 44 moved to Salzburg-Maxglam, Austria on 28 April where it became the IV./JG 7 (13., 14. and 15. Staffeln), a short-lived unit which only carried out one

10. Some sources went even further, even suggesting the Reichsmarschall wanted him to commit suicide…
11. The origins of this designation are still unknown even today. Some evoke Galland harking back to his former group in the Condor legion in Spain, the J./88, with the figure being divided in two.
12. Especially developed for fast interceptors and therefore the jet fighters, the R4M (Rakete, 4 Kilogramm, Minenkopf) "Orkan" was a 55-mm diameter 6 ½-lb (3.5 kg) air-to-air rocket; 24 could be carried by an Me 262 underwing; they were fired in salvoes of six at 2 130 feet (650 m). They had the same trajectory as a 30-mm shell so they could be aimed with the classic Revi sight. Thanks to the 1 lb (520 g) Hexogen explosive charge in the head, each salvo formed a 50-foot (15 m) by 100-foot (30 m) square making a bull's eye almost inevitable and a single rocket was capable of downing a bomber by ripping off one of its wings.

mission on 29 April 1945, with Heinz Bär nonetheless scoring another kill, a P-47! The 25 Schwalbes it still had on 7 May 1945 were deliberately sabotaged by exploding grenades inside the engines to prevent the Americans capturing them.

The KG 51 Edelweiss

As we saw earlier, KG 51 had been chosen to become the first unit equipped with Sturmvogels, the bomber version of the Me 262 and had given rise to the Einsatzkommando Schenk which had been sent urgently to France after the Normandy landings in June 1944. After abandoning its Me 410s in May, the I./KG 51 Gruppe had quickly started training and at the beginning of August it had thirty or so jets. When it finally had its full complement of personnel and materiel for a Gruppe a few weeks later, it settled at Rheine-Westfalen where it recovered machines used earlier by the Kdo Schenk and at once started its combat missions. These intensified during Operation Market Garden in the Netherlands at the end of September with the Me 262s being given the task of supporting the ground troops by bombing various priority targets like the Rhine bridges, missions during which the jets had to face particularly determined Allied fighters which took a heavy tribute.

The II./KG 51, which had also abandoned its Me 410s in August 1944, was sent to Hesepe and Achmer to finish its training and became operational in October. It immediately carried out missions over Belgium and Holland which continued until the end of the year with the KG 51 making more than 300 combat sorties for the months of November and December alone. From the middle of that month, the group was engaged, when the terrible weather conditions permitted, in the final German offensive on the Western Front, in the Ardennes, then took part on 1 January 1945 in Operation Bodenplatte, with 21 of its planes being sent to bomb Eindoven and Hertogenbosch airfields.

In March, the group's various units were forced to move often because of the advancing Allied troops, the II. Gruppe settling at Schwäbisch Hall on 20 March; the I./KG 51 had moved to Giebelstadt a few days earlier. There it was also able to use a portion of the motorway situated near the town of Leipheim. At the end of the same month, all KG 51's Staffeln fell back into Bavaria or into Western Austria and had a large number of Me 262s (nearly eighty) because of the two Messerschmitt factories nearby; this number was not long in plunging

for only ten days later there were only ten left... When the I./KG 51 flew its last mission of the war on 22 April, the II. Gruppe only existed on paper and was finally disbanded the following day on the airfield at Landau-Isar. Its last five operational machines were then transferred to 2./KG 51; this was stationed at Munich-Riem where the group's Me 262s (eight in all) were to be taken on by the JV 44. When this order was rescinded, the 2./KG 51 was sent to Prague on 30 April and incorporated into the "Gefechtsverband Hogeback", in which it carried out mainly ground support missions for the Wehrmacht fighting in the Prague area until the end of the fighting, on 8 May 1945, losing several planes and pilots.

The KG (J) 54 "Totenkopf"

At the end of August 1944, the I. and III./KG 54 "Totenkopf" were recalled from the front to begin their training on the Me 262A-2. Because there weren't enough planes, the group, renamed KG(J) 54 in October to make its new role clear, only began its war missions in mid-December at the time of the Battle of the Bulge with its CO, with Oberst Volprecht Riesedel Freiherr zu Eisenbach reporting that it was in battle order just before the end of 1944 with its 45 Me 262s. Because of the lack of proper training, the Junkers Ju 88 pilots had trouble getting used to the jet fighter which also suffered from frequent breakdowns and other mechanical incidents. And the situation didn't get any better when the KG(J) 54 was launched against the Allied four-engined heavies. Indeed during the first mission of this type on 9 February, out of the 18 Schwalbes launched against the Dicke Autos in terrible weather conditions, six were shot down by the escorting fighters, including that of the Kommodore, and two others on landing...

A few days later, on 25 February, the group suffered a terrible humiliation, losing seven of its sixteen planes launched at the USAAF's B-17s, with four other being destroyed by strafing Allied Fighters, and two others in accidents. Having thus lost almost all their operational capacity, the two Gruppen from KG(J) 54 ceased their combat missions to complete their training. But things didn't get any better since

Opposite.
The last moments of a Schwalbe filmed by the camera gun of an Eighth Air Force fighter. The sweep of the wings is clearly visible. *(US National Archives)*

a thousand bombers at a time, so it was decided to convert former bomber groups into fighter units equipped with Me 262s in order to try and reduce this threat. As the KG 40, which had ruled the Atlantic with its Fw 200 Condors, was no longer any use in this role, its I. Gruppe and a part of the IV (Erg) were amalgamated at the beginning of November 1944 to form the I./KG(J) 40. The pilots began training at the beginning of 1945 but never had the opportunity to carry out the slightest mission because the group was disbanded in February 1945 and no jet fighter was ever delivered to it. The KG 55 "Greif" was renamed KG(J) 55 in November 1944 and should have converted to jets in March of the following year. Its pilots weren't even able to start their training since the planes which had been assigned to them were all destroyed in an American air raid on 23 March and the unit dissolved on 9 April.

The KG(J) 6

The KG(J) 6 was formed at Prague-Ruzyne commanded by one of the best bomber pilots, *Oberst* Hermann Hogeback, but only received its first Me 262s in the middle of March, starting its war missions in April. In fact only the Stab and the III. Gruppe flew jets; the other units used Bf 109s. On 30 April 1945, KG(J) 6's surviving Me 262s were combined with the remnants of KG(J) 51 and 54 and the I (Erg). The KG 1 which had just arrived in Prague formed the "Gefechtsverband Hogeback". This composite unit fought until the last hours of the war, even losing several machines on the eve of the armistice, at first supporting German troops in the Berlin area, and then over the Czech capital and its environs, after a national uprising began against the Nazis on 5 May.

Reconnaissance units

Based at Zerbst, the Nahaufklärungsgruppe 1 (NAGr 1) received

their airfields were attacked several times in March and a number of machines were destroyed on the ground, so much so that after the raid launched against Neugburg-am-Donau on 24 March, the KG(J) 54 was almost non-existent, its groups having lost almost sixty jets on that day alone… the few survivors, as well as the Me 262s from I. Gruppe were then sent to Zerbst, near Magdeburg at the end of the same month, then to Prague in 11 April where the Schwalbes carried out attacks alone into the first days of May.

The results of this group's activities weren't exactly brilliant because although credited with shooting down forty or so enemy aircraft, it didn't produce any aces and above all it had a very high loss rate (almost 70% of 15 machines), mainly because of the fighting, but also in air raids on its bases or due to technical problems.

Other units

By the end of December 1944, the Reich's territory was being constantly pounded day and night, by air raids using more than

Me 262B-1a/U1 (WNr 111980) from 10./NJG 11 photographed in company of some other night-fighter two-seaters on the airfield at Schleswig-Jagel, captured by the Allies and already wearing British roundels. *(US National Archives)*

some Me 262s from February onwards as well as some examples of the jet's reconnaissance version, the Me 262A-1a/U3, with which it carried out several missions until its airfield was captured at the end of the war.

The second reconnaissance unit, the Nahaufklärungsgruppe 6 was formed in the spring of 1944 and equipped at first with Bf 109Gs then Me 262s, especially the reconnaissance version. It was renamed Einsatzkommando Braunegg after its CO, *Hauptmann* Herward Braunegg in November 1944, and carried out a lot of missions over Great Britain and collected precious information in December 1944 during the Battle of the Bulge and in preparation for the massive attack on Allied airfields by the Luftwaffe on 1 January 1945, Operation Bodenplatte. At the time the unit had chosen NAGr 6, its original designation, (comprising the Stab and the 2. Staffel) and carried out reconnaissance missions for the ground troops until the end of hostilities, after being forced to move to Fassberg in the middle of April.

The Industrieschutzstaffeln

At the end of January 1945, the C.-in-C. of the Fighters ordered two small units to be created to protect strategic industrial sites and in particular the factories which produced the Me 262. The Industrieschutzstaffeln 1 (ISS1) and 2 (ISS2), each consisting of six Schwalbe, as many pilots and a hundred or so ground crew settled respectively at Lechfeld and Obertraubling. It's very unlikely these units carried out any war missions since they were amalgamated in February into the JV 44 and JG 7.

The two-seaters and the night fighters

The Me 262 two-seater, or B-1a, was obtained by converting a single-seater (replacing one of the fuselage tanks with the second cockpit, and fitting a new one-piece canopy). According to the initial programme, 65 two-seaters were to be built by Blohm und Voss in Hamburg, and 41 by the Lufthansa workshops. In the end, only 15 examples were produced, the first of them being delivered to the III./EJG 2 at Lechfeld.

In September 1944 while waiting for the real night fighter version (the Me 262B-2a, with a 5-ft (1.5 m) longer fuselage), it was decided to change a few two-seaters into night fighters. These Me 262B-1A/U1s, of which a dozen were produced in the Lufthansa workshops at Berlin-Staaken, kept their standard armament of four 20-mm cannon, and were fitted with suitable equipment for their new role, consisting of a FuG 219 V2 Neptun radar, an IFF FuG 125a/FuG 120 transponder and FuG 25 and FuG 16ZY radios. Although the twin controls were retained, the instrumentation on the other hand for the radar operator at the rear was simplified.

At the end of October 1944, the Kommando Welter, a night-fighter unit equipped with Messerschmitt Bf 109G-10s and G-14s started to receive its Me 262, at first some single-seaters (of which one was equipped with a FuG 226 radar), then two-seaters in February 1945, when the first of seven Me 262B-1a/U1s were delivered. Renamed 10./NJG 11 at the end of February 1945, the unit was able, in spite of its reduced strength and continual lack of fuel, to carry out a large number of missions (160 for April alone) and especially was able to claim 48 kills, mainly against Mosquitoes, with the Staffel's "boss", *Major* Welter alone scoring 29 kills of which two were four-engined heavies.

Operating from its base at Burg-Bei-Magdeburg until April 1945, the Kommando Welter/10./NJG 11 used a portion of the Reinfeld motorway. Out of the twenty or so (23 or 25, of which seven were two-seaters)

Above.
France recovered eight Me 262s including a two-seater but only flight tested three at the Bretigny CEV (Test Centre) in 1947-48 after making them operational. Note the instrumentation probe under the camera gun port. *(ECPAD)*

Above.
After the war, the Czech firm used Me 262 parts produced in the country during the war to build five single-seaters (S-92) and two two-seaters (CS-92) used by the Czech air force.

Above.
One of the Me 262s recovered by the British, seen here on the airfield at Lubeck and already sporting the new owner's roundels

Above.
In order to convert the Me 262 into a bomber, the V10 was used to test the Deich-selschlepp concept, a 1 000 kg bomb equipped with wings (from the V-1) and towed using a rigid rod. This system was just as dangerous as it was ineffective and was quickly abandoned.

Above.
A Lichtenstein SN 2 radar was installed on V56 (WNr 170056) as part of the trials for the single-seat variant of the Schwalbe night fighter, the Me 262A-7a/U2. Note the aerials slanting down at 25°. *(Air Force Museum Collection)*

Above.
Two Me 262A-1/U-4s including this one (WNr 111899) were equipped with MK 214 50-MM cannon located at the front of the fuselage, which meant modifying the nose wheel which now retracted flat into the well. They were used together on two occasions by JV 44 without result.

A QUESTION OF NUMBERS

Although the exact figure will never be known, it is generally admitted that 1 433 examples of the Me 262, all versions and variants included, were delivered to the Luftwaffe but in the end that only half of them were able to reach their combat units. At the end of the war a few hundred machines were left in different stages of assembly. According to an official Messerschmitt document, 10 prototypes and 112 production series machines had been produced as at 10 August 1944. Out of this total, six proto-types and 32 production series machines were destroyed and there were 84 machines available, of which 33 in the KG 54, 15 in the EKdo 262 and 14 at the E-Stelle at Rechlin. On 10 January 1945 more than 500 of the different versions of the Me 262 had been delivered to the Luftwaffe (more than thirty per week), but the Staff could only report ... 60 machines being in the operational units, of which 52 in the I. and II./KG 51. At the end of April 1945, a few days before the conflict ended, about 1 200 jets had been delivered to the Luftwaffe but only 200 were indeed in operational units by 9 April.

Schwalbes, which was its maximum strength, there were only seven (of which three were two-seaters) left when it disbanded on 7 May 1945.

Technical description

FUSELAGE

The Me 262's fuselage had an almost triangular cross-section with rounded angles and with a flat bottom which contributed to increase lift (like the American Lifting Bodies of the Sixties); it was an all-metal, monocoque construction, without spars and covered with aluminium panels. The fuselage was made up of three sections:

— the nose section comprising both the armament and the nose-wheel with its retracting mechanism and its wheel well. A moulded aluminium cone containing a BSK 16 camera gun was bolted to the front partition of this section.

— the central, semi-monocoque section consisted of two parts. The front part was short and contained a self-sealing 199-gallon (900-litre) fuel tank; and the second, just behind the firewall bulkhead, contained the semi-cylindrical, pressurised cockpit "tub". The instrument panel was made of plywood and all the other instruments were placed in side consoles and on the inside right panel (fuses). All the cable and piping ducts in this tub were fitted with seals so they were perfectly air tight for the pressurisation. The cockpit was protected by a three-piece canopy made of synthetic glass with metal frames, the central one swinging up over to the right. The front windshield panel was made of 90-mm thick armoured glass.

The main undercarriage retracted inwards under the cockpit. It had a wide track and the legs were fitted with moulded metal well doors (wood for the nose wheel) which covered them completely when up. Lowering and retracting the undercarriage was done hydraulically with a pneumatic back-up system. All the wheels had brakes.

— The rear section was triangular in shape tapering off into an ellipse. In the front part, just behind the cockpit bulkhead, was the second fuel tank holding 199 gallons (900 litres). A 38-gallon (170-litre) back-up tank was installed under the cockpit, in front of the central wing spar and a fourth tank (132 gallon/600 litres) could be installed in the rear section of the fuselage, though the radio equipment would have to be moved backwards, modifying the plane's centre of gravity. The rear of the fuselage and the tail were a single unit made up of two semi-monocoque sections. The tail's leading edge had a 45° sweep the rudder was all-metal and fitted with a 50-cm trimming tab. On the pre-production series machines, a position light was sunk into the trailing edge.

The cantilever horizontal stabilisers were swept back at 23° and their incidence could be adjusted by means of an electric motor.

WINGS

The swept-back, cantilever wings (18.5°) were attached to the base of the fuselage by means of four gudgeons; they had a single steel spar. They were covered in aluminium alloy and had automatic slats along the whole length of the leading edge, ailerons made of Dural, two-section Fowler-type flaps and a simple slot between the flaps and the wing roots.

POWERPLANTS

These were two Junkers Jumo 109-004B (the B-1 variant usually, but the B-2 and B-3 were also used) slung under the wings. These engines had an eight-stage compressor and a single stage turbine placed along a single axis. The injected fuel was burnt in six combustion chambers, and a mobile cone (called a Zwiebel – onion) in the rear part enabled the flow to be regulated, moving back progressively as the speed increased. In flight, the cone moved automatically controlled by a pressure probe. The outlet temperature was more than 600° and the thrust was 1 760 lbf (800 kgp) at 8 700 rpm.

The engine was started using a Riedel starter located in the front part of the engine fairing. It was a two cylinder, two-stroke engine set off by a starter and fed from a 1/2-gallon (1.5 litre) tank fitted in each of the front nacelle rings. In theory, the Jumo 004B could be operated using three types of fuel: J-2, the most frequently used

and obtained from coal, diesel fuel or aviation fuel which weren't used very much because they increased consumption considerably. Because there weren't enough strategic materials included in its basic design, the engines' life cycle was very short (about ten hours) and breakdowns and even accidents (compressor blades breaking, etc.) were very frequent.

AVIONICS

This was rather simple and consisted mainly of an air-to-air/air-to-ground FuG 16ZY radio and a Friend or Foe FuG 25A transponder. The Revi 16B sights used for the on-board cannon, or even the R4M rockets, were mounted on a retractable support in order to prevent accidents.

ARMAMENT

The armament, including the ammunition cases, was concentrated in the front section of the fuselage and was accessed through two panels opening upwards. On the principal version, the Me 262A-1a, it consisted of four MK 108 cannon with a rate of fire of 600 rounds per minute; the upper pair had a hundred rounds and the lower pair, eighty. Firing was pneumatic with a selector on the joystick, the system being fed by eight air bottles fitted on either side of the armament bay.

The fixed armament could be supplemented by bombs (550-lb /250-Kg SC 250 or 1 100lb/500-kg SC500 bombs) fitted to faired underwing pylons placed just behind the nose wheel well, which could also carry two WGr 21 rocket launching tubes or two extra drop tanks. Towards the end of the war, some units quite successfully used R4M Orkan air-to-air rockets – twelve could be fitted to wooden launchers under each wing. These rockets were launched electromechanically and aiming used the Revi sights in the cockpit. ❏

A famous photograph of Me 262A-2a (WNr 170096) from 1./KG 51 showing the Sturmvogel's characteristic camouflage. The top of the tail and the nose tip are white, the colour of 1. Staffel.

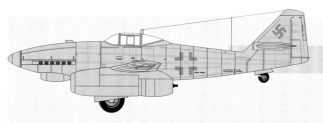

Me 262 V1: Jumo 210G piston engine installed in the nose and two BMW 109003-A turbojets. First flight (with the three engines) on 26 March 1942.

Me 262 V3: two Jumo 109-004A turbojets. 1st flight 18 July 1942.

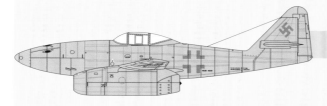

Me 262 V6: first example fitted with retractable undercarriage, first flight 26 June 1943.

Me 262 V9: modified prototype (wings, tail fin and lower, faired canopy) for aerodynamic and high speed trials.

Me 262 V056: single-seat night fighter fitted with FuG 218 Neptun V radar and FuG 226 Neuling friend or foe transponder. 1 example built.

Me 262A-1a: the principal version of the standard production series. 2 Junkers Jumo 109-004B turbojets. Fixed armament: four 20 mm MK 108 cannon.

Me 262A-1a/Jabo (or Bo, or Me 262A-1a/R6): interim fighter-bomber version Fixed armament and identical powerplants but two ETC 503, then ETC 504 pylons added under the front of the fuselage, behind the nose wheel well with a maximum load of 1 000 lb (500 kg) (two 500 lb (250 kg) SC 250 bombs or a single 1 000 lb (500-kg) SC 500 bomb).

Me 262A-1a/U1: heavy fighter with two MG 151/20 cannon with 146 rounds each, two 30 mm MK 108 with 66 rounds each, and two 30 mm MK 103s with 72 rounds each. Two or three examples converted.

Me 262A-1a/U2: "bad weather" fighter, identical to the A-1a with extra radar.

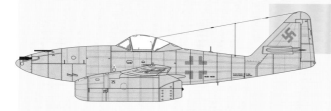

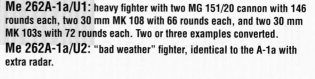

Me 262A-1a/U3: interim reconnaissance machine, fixed armament replaced with cameras (2 Robot Rb 50/30s, or 1 Rb 20/30 and 1 Rb 75/30).

Me 262A-5a: Armed reconnaissance machine, identical to the A-1/U3 but with underwing pylons for drop tanks, extra glazing in the cockpit floor and two MK 108 cannon in the lower part of the fuselage. One built, flight uncertain.

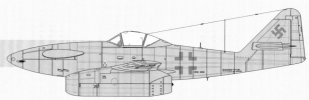

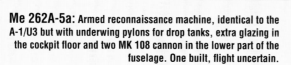

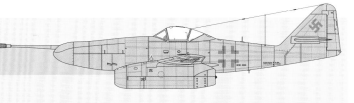

Me 262 A-1a/U4 "Pulkzerstörer": the same as the standard A-1a but armament replaced by 50 mm Mauser MK 214 canon installed in the front part of a modified fuselage, nose-wheel retracting flat. Two examples modified, trials (perhaps in combat for one of them) in April 1945.

Me 262A-1a/U5: heavy fighter equipped with six 20 mm MK 108 cannon (an extra pair under the production series' two pairs). One example converted.

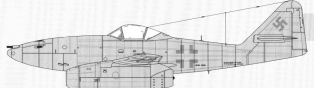

Me 262A-1b: as for the Me 262A-1a but with BMW 003 turbo-jets. 4 examples built.

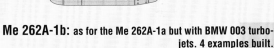

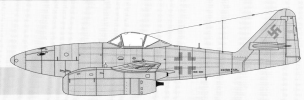

Me 262A-2a "Sturmvogel": fighter-bomber with a single pair of MK 108 cannon in the front, extra fuel tank behind the cockpit and ETC 503/504 pylons under the front part of the fuselage. Take-off weight increased by 325 kg.

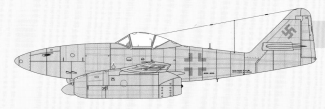

Me 262A-2a/U1: same as the Me 262A-1a but TSA-2A sights increasing accuracy by 400%. 3 planes modified and tried out.

Me 262A-2a/U2: two seat bomber with the second crewman lying down in the nose and using Lofte 7H sights. 2 examples built.

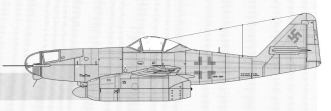

Me 262B-1a: two-seater obtained by converting a single-seater, replacing the fuselage tank with the second cockpit and twin controls and a new one-piece canopy opening to the right. Fifteen built.

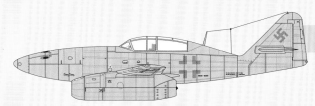

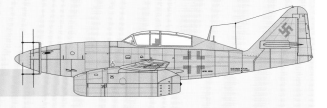

Me 262B-1a/U1: two-seat interim night fighter version while waiting for the production series version to arrive (Me 262B-2a with fuselage lengthened by 5 ft (1.50 m) obtained by converting the two-seat training version). Fixed armament (four 20 mm cannon) retained and new equipment comprising a FuG 218 Neptun V radar, an IFF FuG 25a transponder, a FuG 350 ZC detector copied off the British H2S radar, and FuG 16ZY R/T and FuG 120a Bernardine radios.

Me 262C-1a ("Heimatschützer"): like the standard Me 262 but equipped with a Walter HWK 109-509-A2 rocket (like the Me 163B's) installed at the rear of the fuselage. One example made (WNr 130186). 1st flight 27 February 1945.

Me 262C-2b: two BMW 003-A3 turbojets and one BMW 109-718 rocket giving 2 200 lb (1 000 kg) of thrust for three minutes, fitted below the rear of the fuselage and using synthetic fuels (SV Stoff - concentrated nitric acid, and R Stoff - "Tonka"). 1 example (WNr 170078) made a test flight but was abandoned for the:

Me 262C-3a: exactly the same but with a Walter 109-509A-2 jettisonable rocket. Not produced.

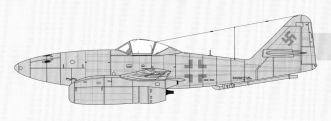

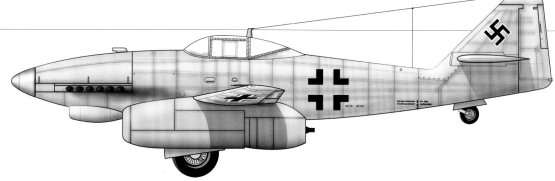

Messerschmitt Me 262 V1 (WNr 26200001), Leipheim, March 1942. Because there were no engines available, the V1 only flew after 18 April 1941 using a single Jumo 210G piston engine. When it finally received its BMW turbojets at the beginning of the following year, it took to the air for the first time in this new configuration on 25 March 1942, piloted by Fritz Wendel.

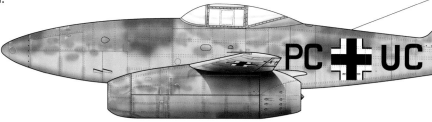

Messerschmitt Me 262 V3 (WNr 26200003). Augsburg, July 1942. The V3 was the first Me 262 prototype to fly using its own Jumo 004A-0 turbojets, on 17 July 1942, piloted by Fritz Wendel. Badly damaged at Rechlin on the following 11 August, it was repaired and carried out a total of 149 test flights before it was almost completely destroyed during an air raid on Lechfeld on 12 September 1944.

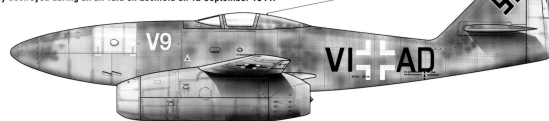

Messerschmitt Me 262 V9 (WNr 130004), Lechfeld, spring 1944. The ninth prototype of the Me 262 was considerably modified at the beginning of 1944, to increase its performance as part of the HG 1 (HochGeschwindigkeit/high speed) programme, fitted with a more faired canopy ("Rennkabine" or racing canopy). During the aerodynamic trials, carried out together with the V12, the V9 reached the speed of 1 004 kph in a shallow dive on 6 June 1944

Messerschmitt Me 262 S7 (WNr 130012) from the EKdo 262, Lechfeld, June 1944. Delivered in May 1944, this plane, painted entirely RLM 76 light grey, crashed on 1 June following a fire in one of the engines. Although this is the seventh production series example, it bears the individual number "6" because it was the 6th machine to be delivered to the EKdo 262.

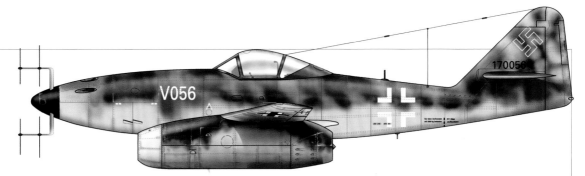

Messerschmitt Me 262A-1a (WNr 170056), Lechfeld, beginning of 1945. Renamed "V056", this was the prototype of the single-seat nightfighter variant, the A-1a/U2. Kept by Messerschmitt, this example made its first flight in July 1944 and then was used for several tests, its first flight with complete night-fighter equipment and especially its Hirschgeweih (antlers) antennae at the front, only taking place on 9 March 1945.

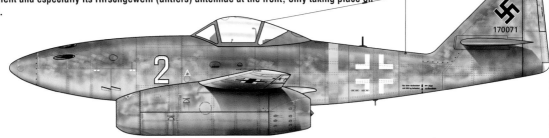

Messerschmitt Me 262A-1a (WNr 170071) from the EKdo 262, Lechfeld, August 1944. Visible in the foreground on several period photographs of the EKdo 262 Schwalbes, this machine which uses the first type of camouflage scheme was delivered to the III./EJG 2 and used by Major Erich Hohagen before in the end being abandoned in May 1945

Messerschmitt Me 262A-1a (WNr 170045) from the EKdo 262, Lechfeld, summer of 1944. It was aboard this machine that Leutnant Joachim Weber intercepted an RAF Mosquito PR XVI on 8 August 1944, thus scoring the only confirmed kill by the EKdo 262.

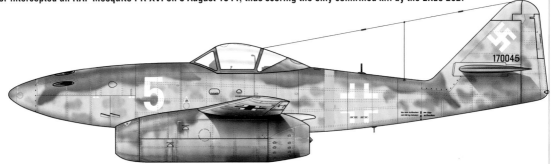

Messerschmitt Me 262A-1a (WNr 170067) from the Erprobungskommando (EKdo) 262, Lechfeld, August 1944. This machine is visible on a period photograph in an eight-Schwalbes line up in the company of "White 2" and "White 5".

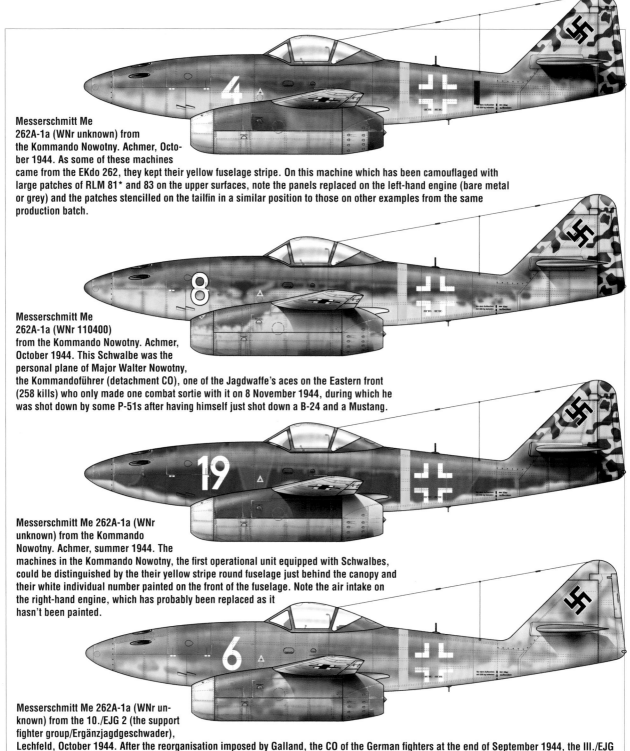

Messerschmitt Me
262A-1a (WNr unknown) from
the Kommando Nowotny. Achmer, October 1944. As some of these machines
came from the EKdo 262, they kept their yellow fuselage stripe. On this machine which has been camouflaged with
large patches of RLM 81* and 83 on the upper surfaces, note the panels replaced on the left-hand engine (bare metal
or grey) and the patches stencilled on the tailfin in a similar position to those on other examples from the same
production batch.

Messerschmitt Me
262A-1a (WNr 110400)
from the Kommando Nowotny. Achmer,
October 1944. This Schwalbe was the
personal plane of Major Walter Nowotny,
the Kommandoführer (detachment CO), one of the Jagdwaffe's aces on the Eastern front
(258 kills) who only made one combat sortie with it on 8 November 1944, during which he
was shot down by some P-51s after having himself just shot down a B-24 and a Mustang.

Messerschmitt Me 262A-1a (WNr
unknown) from the Kommando
Nowotny. Achmer, summer 1944. The
machines in the Kommando Nowotny, the first operational unit equipped with Schwalbes,
could be distinguished by the their yellow stripe round fuselage just behind the canopy and
their white individual number painted on the front of the fuselage. Note the air intake on
the right-hand engine, which has probably been replaced as it
hasn't been painted.

Messerschmitt Me 262A-1a (WNr unknown) from the 10./EJG 2 (the support
fighter group/Ergänzjagdgeschwader),
Lechfeld, October 1944. After the reorganisation imposed by Galland, the CO of the German fighters at the end of September 1944, the III./EJG
2 was officially given the job of training Schwalbe pilots. It therefore recovered a large number of already delivered machines and maintained
the yellow 11-inch (30-cm) wide fuselage stripe painted just behind the canopy.

* RLM 81 is a colour which is the subject of controversy, authors being incapable of agreeing on its official designation: Dunkelbraun (dark brown), Braunviolett (violet brown), Dunkelgrün (dark
green) or Olivbraun (olive brown)... It seems than in reality the shade of RLM 81 varied depending on the origins of its paint, ranging from reddish brown to the official Violet to Dark green. As far
as we are concerned we have chosen the first option for our profiles mainly to show this colour up when it is combined with others.

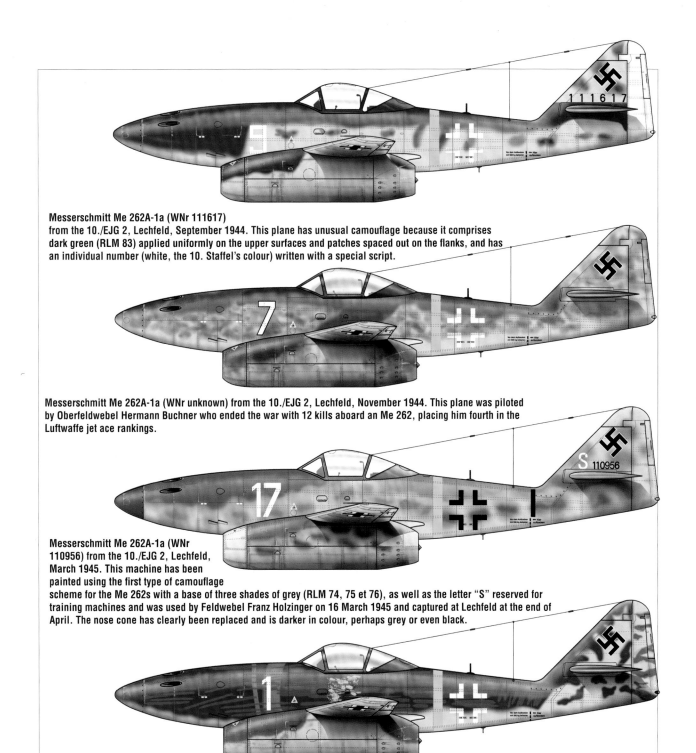

Messerschmitt Me 262A-1a (WNr 111617) from the 10./EJG 2, Lechfeld, September 1944. This plane has unusual camouflage because it comprises dark green (RLM 83) applied uniformly on the upper surfaces and patches spaced out on the flanks, and has an individual number (white, the 10. Staffel's colour) written with a special script.

Messerschmitt Me 262A-1a (WNr unknown) from the 10./EJG 2, Lechfeld, November 1944. This plane was piloted by Oberfeldwebel Hermann Buchner who ended the war with 12 kills aboard an Me 262, placing him fourth in the Luftwaffe jet ace rankings.

Messerschmitt Me 262A-1a (WNr 110956) from the 10./EJG 2, Lechfeld, March 1945. This machine has been painted using the first type of camouflage scheme for the Me 262s with a base of three shades of grey (RLM 74, 75 et 76), as well as the letter "S" reserved for training machines and was used by Feldwebel Franz Holzinger on 16 March 1945 and captured at Lechfeld at the end of April. The nose cone has clearly been replaced and is darker in colour, perhaps grey or even black.

Messerschmitt Me 262A-1a (WNr unknown) from the EJG 2, Austria, May 1945. Camouflaged with RLM 82 green on the upper surfaces and RLM 76 pale grey underneath with extra patches of RLM 81, this plane has a similar tail to those of the JG 7 machines, with stencilled patches painted.

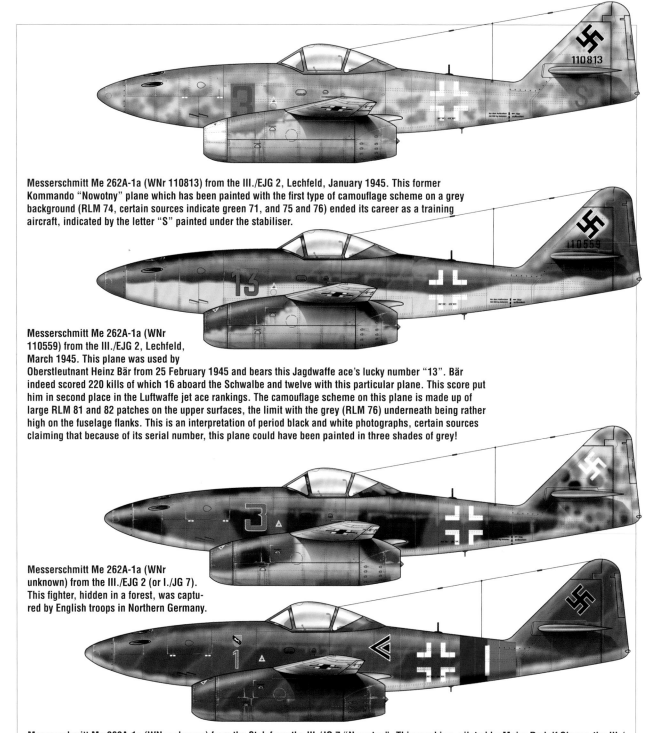

Messerschmitt Me 262A-1a (WNr 110813) from the III./EJG 2, Lechfeld, January 1945. This former Kommando "Nowotny" plane which has been painted with the first type of camouflage scheme on a grey background (RLM 74, certain sources indicate green 71, and 75 and 76) ended its career as a training aircraft, indicated by the letter "S" painted under the stabiliser.

Messerschmitt Me 262A-1a (WNr 110559) from the III./EJG 2, Lechfeld, March 1945. This plane was used by Oberstleutnant Heinz Bär from 25 February 1945 and bears this Jagdwaffe ace's lucky number "13". Bär indeed scored 220 kills of which 16 aboard the Schwalbe and twelve with this particular plane. This score put him in second place in the Luftwaffe jet ace rankings. The camouflage scheme on this plane is made up of large RLM 81 and 82 patches on the upper surfaces, the limit with the grey (RLM 76) underneath being rather high on the fuselage flanks. This is an interpretation of period black and white photographs, certain sources claiming that because of its serial number, this plane could have been painted in three shades of grey!

Messerschmitt Me 262A-1a (WNr unknown) from the III./EJG 2 (or I./JG 7). This fighter, hidden in a forest, was captured by English troops in Northern Germany.

Messerschmitt Me 262A-1a (WNr unknown) from the Stab from the III./JG 7 "Nowotny". This machine, piloted by Major Rudolf Sinner, the III./JG 7's Gruppenkommandeur, as the double chevron on the fuselage indicates, has been camouflaged with large diagonal stripes of RLM 81 and 82, and RLM 76 on the undersides. Sinner was seriously wounded aboard this plane during an attack by P-51s on 4 April 1945, as he was taking off from his airfield.

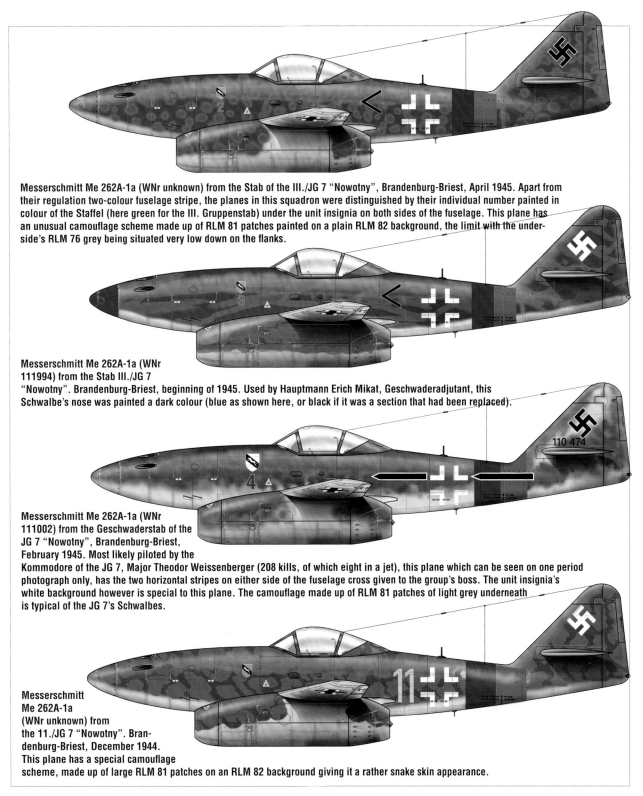

Messerschmitt Me 262A-1a (WNr unknown) from the Stab of the III./JG 7 "Nowotny", Brandenburg-Briest, April 1945. Apart from their regulation two-colour fuselage stripe, the planes in this squadron were distinguished by their individual number painted in colour of the Staffel (here green for the III. Gruppenstab) under the unit insignia on both sides of the fuselage. This plane has an unusual camouflage scheme made up of RLM 81 patches painted on a plain RLM 82 background, the limit with the underside's RLM 76 grey being situated very low down on the flanks.

Messerschmitt Me 262A-1a (WNr 111994) from the Stab III./JG 7 "Nowotny". Brandenburg-Briest, beginning of 1945. Used by Hauptmann Erich Mikat, Geschwaderadjutant, this Schwalbe's nose was painted a dark colour (blue as shown here, or black if it was a section that had been replaced).

Messerschmitt Me 262A-1a (WNr 111002) from the Geschwaderstab of the JG 7 "Nowotny", Brandenburg-Briest, February 1945. Most likely piloted by the Kommodore of the JG 7, Major Theodor Weissenberger (208 kills, of which eight in a jet), this plane which can be seen on one period photograph only, has the two horizontal stripes on either side of the fuselage cross given to the group's boss. The unit insignia's white background however is special to this plane. The camouflage made up of RLM 81 patches of light grey underneath is typical of the JG 7's Schwalbes.

Messerschmitt Me 262A-1a (WNr unknown) from the 11./JG 7 "Nowotny". Brandenburg-Briest, December 1944. This plane has a special camouflage scheme, made up of large RLM 81 patches on an RLM 82 background giving it a rather snake skin appearance.

25

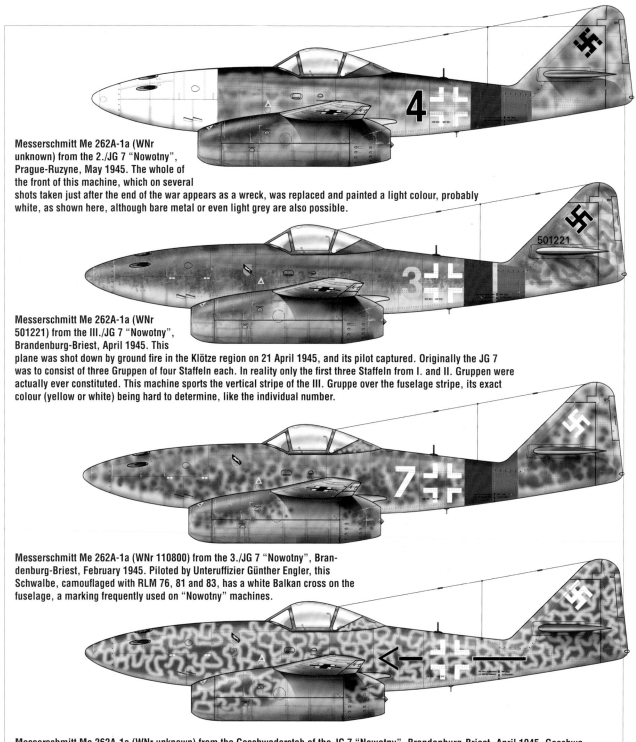

Messerschmitt Me 262A-1a (WNr unknown) from the 2./JG 7 "Nowotny", Prague-Ruzyne, May 1945. The whole of the front of this machine, which on several shots taken just after the end of the war appears as a wreck, was replaced and painted a light colour, probably white, as shown here, although bare metal or even light grey are also possible.

Messerschmitt Me 262A-1a (WNr 501221) from the III./JG 7 "Nowotny", Brandenburg-Briest, April 1945. This plane was shot down by ground fire in the Klötze region on 21 April 1945, and its pilot captured. Originally the JG 7 was to consist of three Gruppen of four Staffeln each. In reality only the first three Staffeln from I. and II. Gruppen were actually ever constituted. This machine sports the vertical stripe of the III. Gruppe over the fuselage stripe, its exact colour (yellow or white) being hard to determine, like the individual number.

Messerschmitt Me 262A-1a (WNr 110800) from the 3./JG 7 "Nowotny", Bran-denburg-Briest, February 1945. Piloted by Unteruffizier Günther Engler, this Schwalbe, camouflaged with RLM 76, 81 and 83, has a white Balkan cross on the fuselage, a marking frequently used on "Nowotny" machines.

Messerschmitt Me 262A-1a (WNr unknown) from the Geschwaderstab of the JG 7 "Nowotny", Brandenburg-Briest, April 1945. Geschwa-derkommodore Theodor Weissenberger might have used this plane. It is camouflaged with RLM 72 curls (over a general background of RLM 76), which was unusual in this group; at the same time it didn't have the red and blue fuselage stripe usually attributed to the "Nowotny".

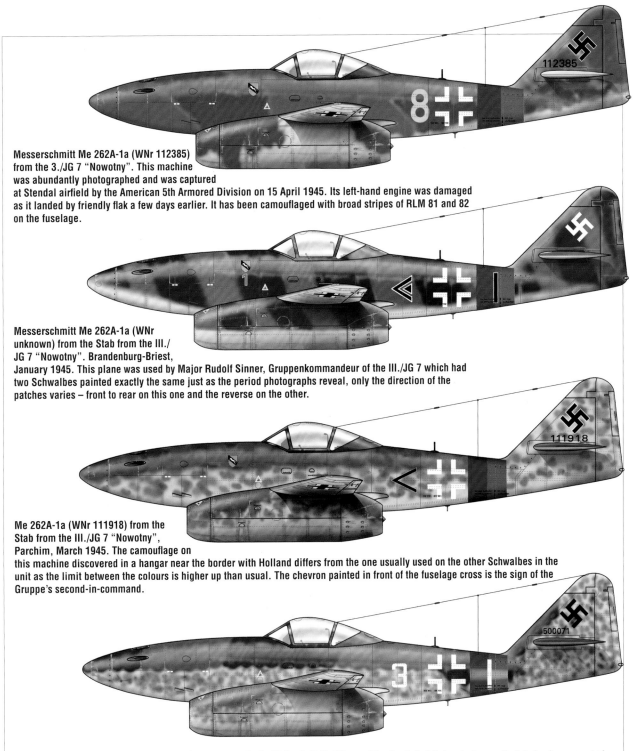

Messerschmitt Me 262A-1a (WNr 112385) from the 3./JG 7 "Nowotny". This machine was abundantly photographed and was captured at Stendal airfield by the American 5th Armored Division on 15 April 1945. Its left-hand engine was damaged as it landed by friendly flak a few days earlier. It has been camouflaged with broad stripes of RLM 81 and 82 on the fuselage.

Messerschmitt Me 262A-1a (WNr unknown) from the Stab from the III./ JG 7 "Nowotny". Brandenburg-Briest, January 1945. This plane was used by Major Rudolf Sinner, Gruppenkommandeur of the III./JG 7 which had two Schwalbes painted exactly the same just as the period photographs reveal, only the direction of the patches varies – front to rear on this one and the reverse on the other.

Me 262A-1a (WNr 111918) from the Stab from the III./JG 7 "Nowotny", Parchim, March 1945. The camouflage on this machine discovered in a hangar near the border with Holland differs from the one usually used on the other Schwalbes in the unit as the limit between the colours is higher up than usual. The chevron painted in front of the fuselage cross is the sign of the Gruppe's second-in-command.

Me 262A-1b (WNr 500071) from the III./JG 7 "Nowotny". On 25 April 1945, this machine landed at Dubendorf, near Zurich, having run out of fuel and its pilot, Fähnrich Hans Guido Mutke, surrendered to Swiss troops. The Schwalbe remained in the country until 1957, when it was given to the Deutsches Museum in Munich where it is now on display in its original livery.

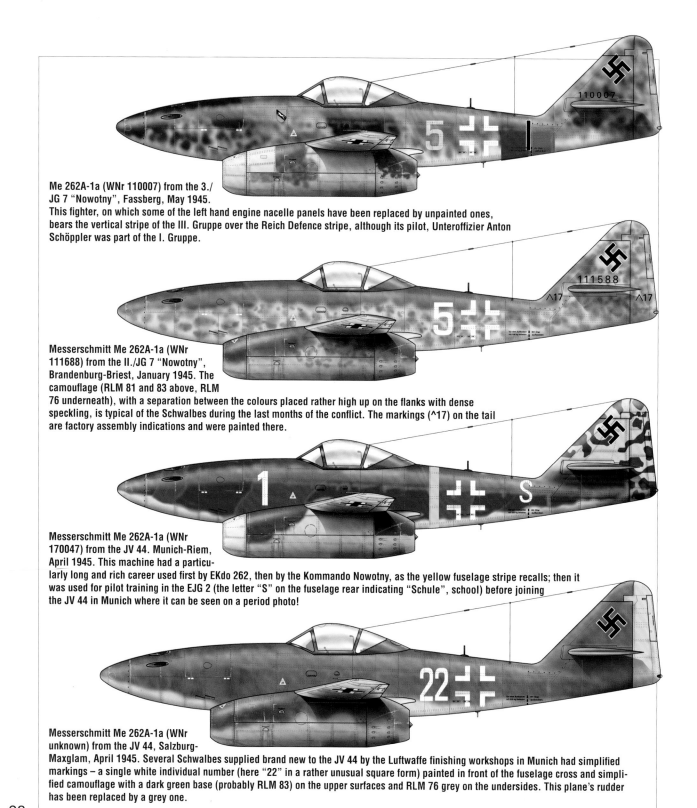

Me 262A-1a (WNr 110007) from the 3./
JG 7 "Nowotny", Fassberg, May 1945.
This fighter, on which some of the left hand engine nacelle panels have been replaced by unpainted ones,
bears the vertical stripe of the III. Gruppe over the Reich Defence stripe, although its pilot, Unteroffizier Anton
Schöppler was part of the I. Gruppe.

Messerschmitt Me 262A-1a (WNr
111688) from the II./JG 7 "Nowotny",
Brandenburg-Briest, January 1945. The
camouflage (RLM 81 and 83 above, RLM
76 underneath), with a separation between the colours placed rather high up on the flanks with dense
speckling, is typical of the Schwalbes during the last months of the conflict. The markings (^17) on the tail
are factory assembly indications and were painted there.

Messerschmitt Me 262A-1a (WNr
170047) from the JV 44. Munich-Riem,
April 1945. This machine had a particu-
larly long and rich career used first by EKdo 262, then by the Kommando Nowotny, as the yellow fuselage stripe recalls; then it
was used for pilot training in the EJG 2 (the letter "S" on the fuselage rear indicating "Schule", school) before joining
the JV 44 in Munich where it can be seen on a period photo!

Messerschmitt Me 262A-1a (WNr
unknown) from the JV 44, Salzburg-
Maxglam, April 1945. Several Schwalbes supplied brand new to the JV 44 by the Luftwaffe finishing workshops in Munich had simplified
markings – a single white individual number (here "22" in a rather unusual square form) painted in front of the fuselage cross and simplified camouflage with a dark green base (probably RLM 83) on the upper surfaces and RLM 76 grey on the undersides. This plane's rudder
has been replaced by a grey one.

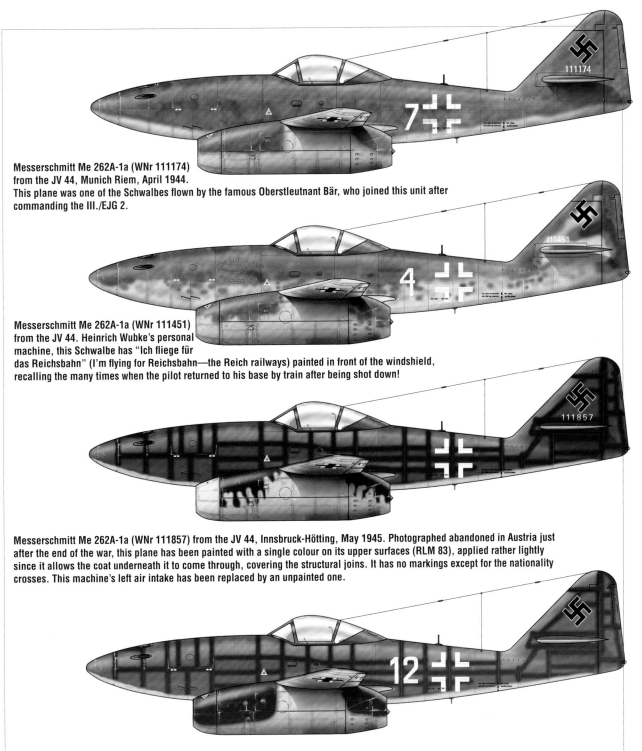

Messerschmitt Me 262A-1a (WNr 111174)
from the JV 44, Munich Riem, April 1944.
This plane was one of the Schwalbes flown by the famous Oberstleutnant Bär, who joined this unit after
commanding the III./EJG 2.

Messerschmitt Me 262A-1a (WNr 111451)
from the JV 44. Heinrich Wubke's personal
machine, this Schwalbe has "Ich fliege für
das Reichsbahn" (I'm flying for Reichsbahn—the Reich railways) painted in front of the windshield,
recalling the many times when the pilot returned to his base by train after being shot down!

Messerschmitt Me 262A-1a (WNr 111857) from the JV 44, Innsbruck-Hötting, May 1945. Photographed abandoned in Austria just
after the end of the war, this plane has been painted with a single colour on its upper surfaces (RLM 83), applied rather lightly
since it allows the coat underneath it to come through, covering the structural joins. It has no markings except for the nationality
crosses. This machine's left air intake has been replaced by an unpainted one.

Messerschmitt Me 262A-1a (WNr unknown) from the JV 44. This Schwalbe was one of the aircraft abandoned in Austria at the armistice; it had been delivered brand new to the JV 44 when it was based at Munich.

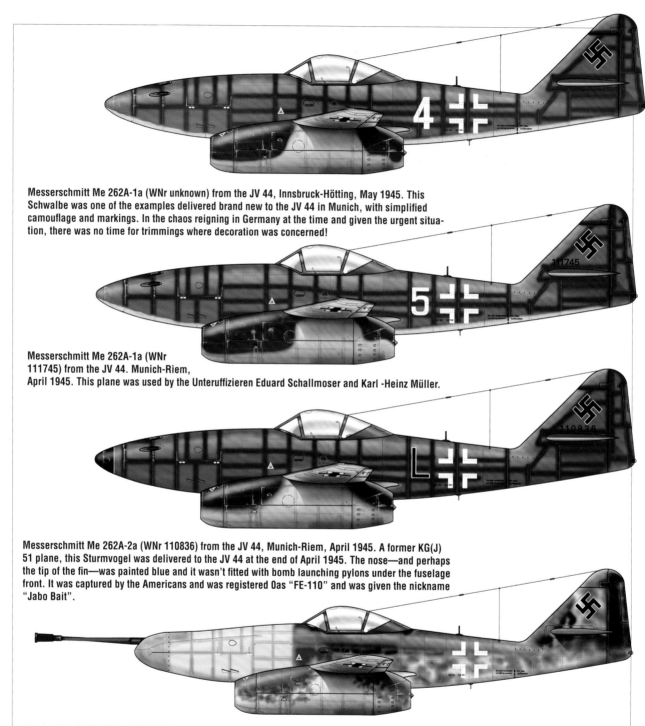

Messerschmitt Me 262A-1a (WNr unknown) from the JV 44, Innsbruck-Hötting, May 1945. This Schwalbe was one of the examples delivered brand new to the JV 44 in Munich, with simplified camouflage and markings. In the chaos reigning in Germany at the time and given the urgent situation, there was no time for trimmings where decoration was concerned!

Messerschmitt Me 262A-1a (WNr 111745) from the JV 44. Munich-Riem, April 1945. This plane was used by the Unteruffizieren Eduard Schallmoser and Karl -Heinz Müller.

Messerschmitt Me 262A-2a (WNr 110836) from the JV 44, Munich-Riem, April 1945. A former KG(J) 51 plane, this Sturmvogel was delivered to the JV 44 at the end of April 1945. The nose—and perhaps the tip of the fin—was painted blue and it wasn't fitted with bomb launching pylons under the fuselage front. It was captured by the Americans and was registered Oas "FE-110" and was given the nickname "Jabo Bait".

Messerschmitt Me 262A-1a/U4 (WNr 111899). At least two fighters were converted into Pulkzerstörer (formation destroyers) armed with a 50-mm Mauser MK 214 canon housed in the front of the fuselage, unpainted here, and sticking out two metres. After trials at Lechfeld, this plane was delivered to the JV 44 based at Munich-Riem and used unsuccessfully in combat, with the second example having no operational career whatsoever.

30

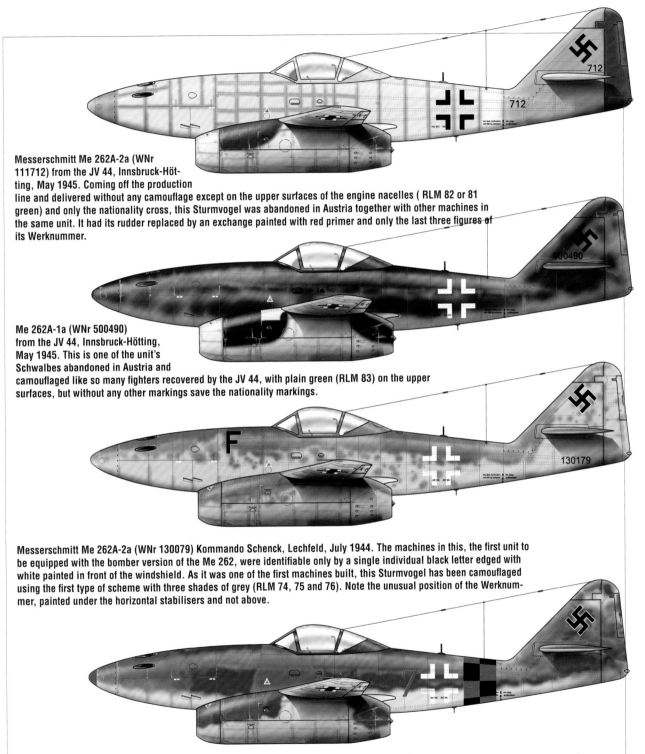

Messerschmitt Me 262A-2a (WNr
111712) from the JV 44, Innsbruck-Hötting, May 1945. Coming off the production
line and delivered without any camouflage except on the upper surfaces of the engine nacelles (RLM 82 or 81
green) and only the nationality cross, this Sturmvogel was abandoned in Austria together with other machines in
the same unit. It had its rudder replaced by an exchange painted with red primer and only the last three figures of
its Werknummer.

Me 262A-1a (WNr 500490)
from the JV 44, Innsbruck-Hötting,
May 1945. This is one of the unit's
Schwalbes abandoned in Austria and
camouflaged like so many fighters recovered by the JV 44, with plain green (RLM 83) on the upper
surfaces, but without any other markings save the nationality markings.

Messerschmitt Me 262A-2a (WNr 130079) Kommando Schenck, Lechfeld, July 1944. The machines in this, the first unit to
be equipped with the bomber version of the Me 262, were identifiable only by a single individual black letter edged with
white painted in front of the windshield. As it was one of the first machines built, this Sturmvogel has been camouflaged
using the first type of scheme with three shades of grey (RLM 74, 75 and 76). Note the unusual position of the Werknummer, painted under the horizontal stabilisers and not above.

Messerschmitt Me 262 A-1a (WNr unknown) from the 8./KG(J) 6. Prague-Ruzine, April 1945. Used regularly by Oberfeldwebel Franz Gaap,
this Me 262 was abandoned on Saatz (Zatec) airfield in Czechoslovakia at the Armistice.

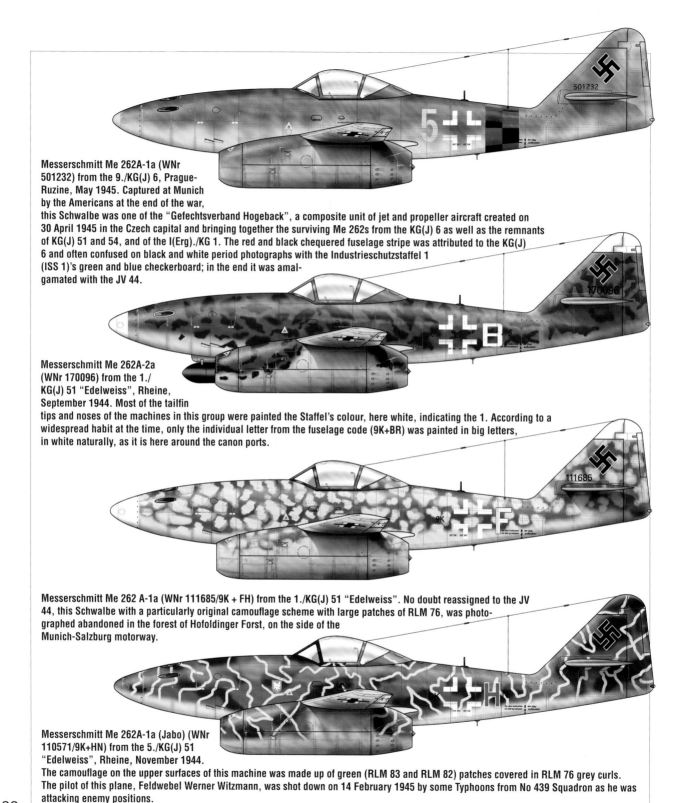

Messerschmitt Me 262A-1a (WNr 501232) from the 9./KG(J) 6, Prague-Ruzine, May 1945. Captured at Munich by the Americans at the end of the war, this Schwalbe was one of the "Gefechtsverband Hogeback", a composite unit of jet and propeller aircraft created on 30 April 1945 in the Czech capital and bringing together the surviving Me 262s from the KG(J) 6 as well as the remnants of KG(J) 51 and 54, and of the I(Erg)./KG 1. The red and black chequered fuselage stripe was attributed to the KG(J) 6 and often confused on black and white period photographs with the Industrieschutzstaffel 1 (ISS 1)'s green and blue checkerboard; in the end it was amalgamated with the JV 44.

Messerschmitt Me 262A-2a (WNr 170096) from the 1./KG(J) 51 "Edelweiss", Rheine, September 1944. Most of the tailfin tips and noses of the machines in this group were painted the Staffel's colour, here white, indicating the 1. According to a widespread habit at the time, only the individual letter from the fuselage code (9K+BR) was painted in big letters, in white naturally, as it is here around the canon ports.

Messerschmitt Me 262 A-1a (WNr 111685/9K + FH) from the 1./KG(J) 51 "Edelweiss". No doubt reassigned to the JV 44, this Schwalbe with a particularly original camouflage scheme with large patches of RLM 76, was photographed abandoned in the forest of Hofoldinger Forst, on the side of the Munich-Salzburg motorway.

Messerschmitt Me 262A-1a (Jabo) (WNr 110571/9K+HN) from the 5./KG(J) 51 "Edelweiss", Rheine, November 1944.
The camouflage on the upper surfaces of this machine was made up of green (RLM 83 and RLM 82) patches covered in RLM 76 grey curls. The pilot of this plane, Feldwebel Werner Witzmann, was shot down on 14 February 1945 by some Typhoons from No 439 Squadron as he was attacking enemy positions.

32

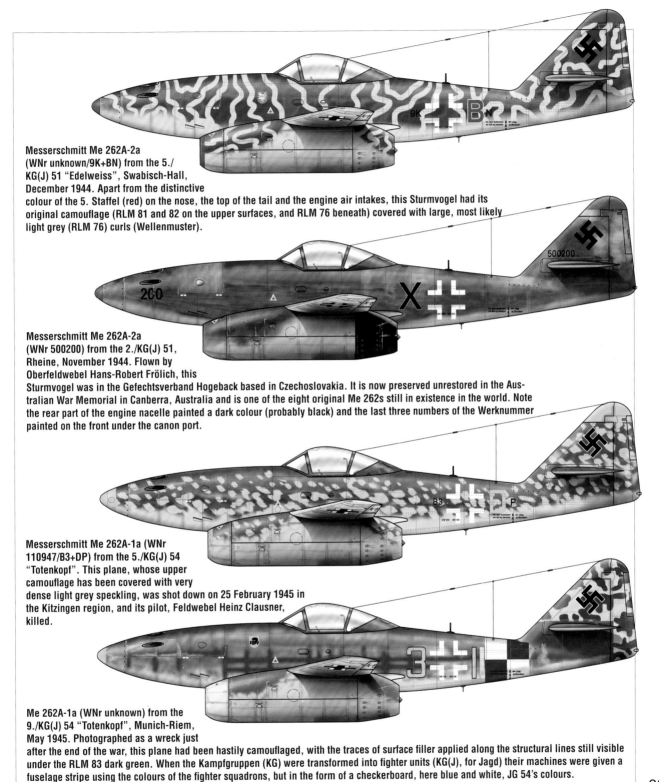

Messerschmitt Me 262A-2a
(WNr unknown/9K+BN) from the 5./
KG(J) 51 "Edelweiss", Swabisch-Hall,
December 1944. Apart from the distinctive
colour of the 5. Staffel (red) on the nose, the top of the tail and the engine air intakes, this Sturmvogel had its
original camouflage (RLM 81 and 82 on the upper surfaces, and RLM 76 beneath) covered with large, most likely
light grey (RLM 76) curls (Wellenmuster).

Messerschmitt Me 262A-2a
(WNr 500200) from the 2./KG(J) 51,
Rheine, November 1944. Flown by
Oberfeldwebel Hans-Robert Frölich, this
Sturmvogel was in the Gefechtsverband Hogeback based in Czechoslovakia. It is now preserved unrestored in the Aus-
tralian War Memorial in Canberra, Australia and is one of the eight original Me 262s still in existence in the world. Note
the rear part of the engine nacelle painted a dark colour (probably black) and the last three numbers of the Werknummer
painted on the front under the canon port.

Messerschmitt Me 262A-1a (WNr
110947/B3+DP) from the 5./KG(J) 54
"Totenkopf". This plane, whose upper
camouflage has been covered with very
dense light grey speckling, was shot down on 25 February 1945 in
the Kitzingen region, and its pilot, Feldwebel Heinz Clausner,
killed.

Me 262A-1a (WNr unknown) from the
9./KG(J) 54 "Totenkopf", Munich-Riem,
May 1945. Photographed as a wreck just
after the end of the war, this plane had been hastily camouflaged, with the traces of surface filler applied along the structural lines still visible
under the RLM 83 dark green. When the Kampfgruppen (KG) were transformed into fighter units (KG(J), for Jagd) their machines were given a
fuselage stripe using the colours of the fighter squadrons, but in the form of a checkerboard, here blue and white, JG 54's colours.

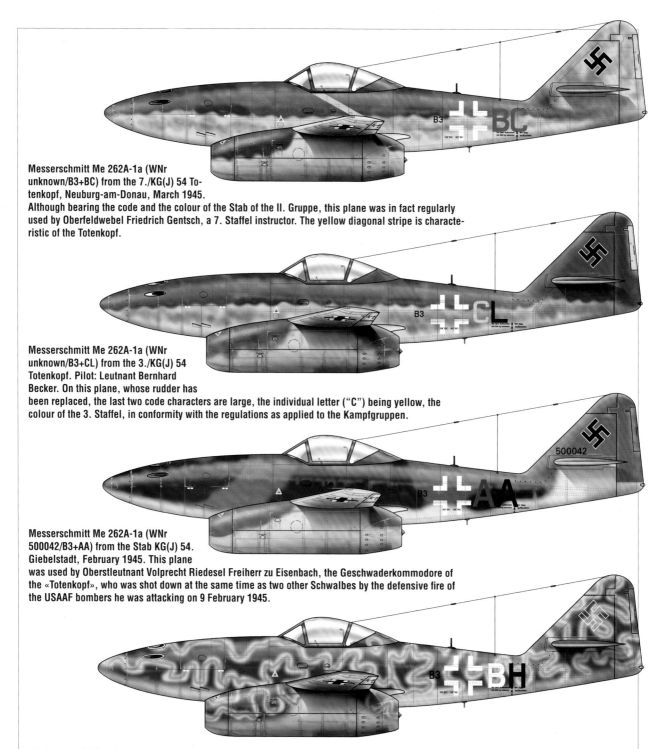

Messerschmitt Me 262A-1a (WNr unknown/B3+BC) from the 7./KG(J) 54 Totenkopf, Neuburg-am-Donau, March 1945.
Although bearing the code and the colour of the Stab of the II. Gruppe, this plane was in fact regularly used by Oberfeldwebel Friedrich Gentsch, a 7. Staffel instructor. The yellow diagonal stripe is characteristic of the Totenkopf.

Messerschmitt Me 262A-1a (WNr unknown/B3+CL) from the 3./KG(J) 54 Totenkopf. Pilot: Leutnant Bernhard Becker. On this plane, whose rudder has been replaced, the last two code characters are large, the individual letter ("C") being yellow, the colour of the 3. Staffel, in conformity with the regulations as applied to the Kampfgruppen.

Messerschmitt Me 262A-1a (WNr 500042/B3+AA) from the Stab KG(J) 54. Giebelstadt, February 1945. This plane was used by Oberstleutnant Volprecht Riedesel Freiherr zu Eisenbach, the Geschwaderkommodore of the «Totenkopf», who was shot down at the same time as two other Schwalbes by the defensive fire of the USAAF bombers he was attacking on 9 February 1945.

Me 262A-2a (WNr unknown/B3+BH) from the 1./KG(J) 54 "Totenkopf", Neuburg-am-Donau, beginning of 1945. This Sturmvogel's upper surfaces have been painted in dark green (RLM 83, or possibly RLM 81) covered with grey (RLM 76) and green twirls.

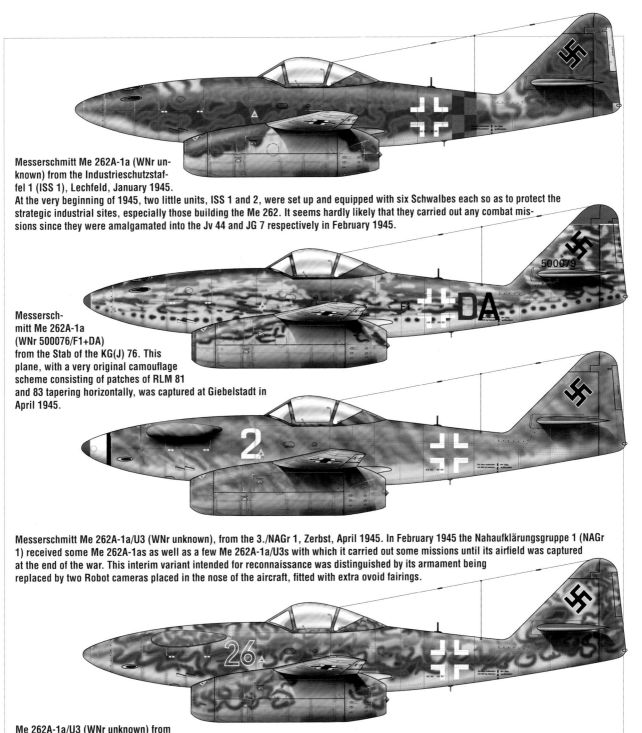

Messerschmitt Me 262A-1a (WNr unknown) from the Industrieschutzstaffel 1 (ISS 1), Lechfeld, January 1945.
At the very beginning of 1945, two little units, ISS 1 and 2, were set up and equipped with six Schwalbes each so as to protect the strategic industrial sites, especially those building the Me 262. It seems hardly likely that they carried out any combat missions since they were amalgamated into the Jv 44 and JG 7 respectively in February 1945.

Messerschmitt Me 262A-1a (WNr 500076/F1+DA) from the Stab of the KG(J) 76. This plane, with a very original camouflage scheme consisting of patches of RLM 81 and 83 tapering horizontally, was captured at Giebelstadt in April 1945.

Messerschmitt Me 262A-1a/U3 (WNr unknown), from the 3./NAGr 1, Zerbst, April 1945. In February 1945 the Nahaufklärungsgruppe 1 (NAGr 1) received some Me 262A-1as as well as a few Me 262A-1a/U3s with which it carried out some missions until its airfield was captured at the end of the war. This interim variant intended for reconnaissance was distinguished by its armament being replaced by two Robot cameras placed in the nose of the aircraft, fitted with extra ovoid fairings.

Me 262A-1a/U3 (WNr unknown) from the 2./NAGr 6, Lechfeld, April 1945. The NAGr 6, made up of two Staffeln, was also called "Kommando Braunegg" after its CO Hauptmann Herward Braunegg, who was in command in March-April 1945. The unit's planes, most of the time variants fitted with cameras, had a special camouflage with the upper surfaces, as here, covered with RLM 82 and 81 patches or twists on a pale grey (RLM 76) background, the only colour applied in the factory.

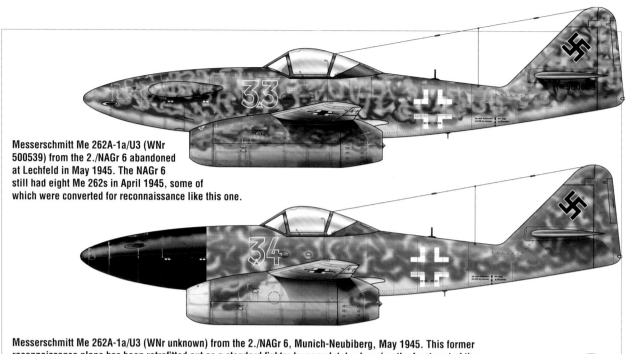

Messerschmitt Me 262A-1a/U3 (WNr 500539) from the 2./NAGr 6 abandoned at Lechfeld in May 1945. The NAGr 6 still had eight Me 262s in April 1945, some of which were converted for reconnaissance like this one.

Messerschmitt Me 262A-1a/U3 (WNr unknown) from the 2./NAGr 6, Munich-Neubiberg, May 1945. This former reconnaissance plane has been retrofitted out as a standard fighter by completely changing the front part of the fuselage—which explains why it is a different shade (black or RLM 81, with the tip RLM 83 green).

Messerschmitt Me 262A-1a (WNr unknown) from the 10./NAGr 11. This machine was found by the Allies at Burg, near Magdeburg where the former Kommando Welter had settled with single-seat Me 262s (about twenty) and two-seaters B-1as (seven). It was used by Feldwebel Karl-Heinz Becker, with seven confirmed kills on Schwalbe. The 10./NAGr 11 also carried out night time missions so this plane with its rather uncommon camouflage scheme (RLM 81 or 83, and 82) had its lower surfaces painted black (RLM 22).

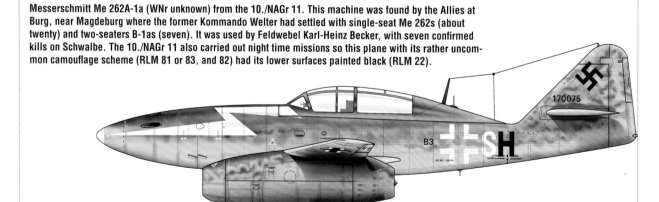

Messerschmitt Me 262B-1 (WNr 170075/B3+SH) from the 1./KG(J) 54, Giebelstadt, November 1944. The white lightning flash (the Staffel's colour) painted on the front of the fuselage is a unique feature on this machine from a period photograph.

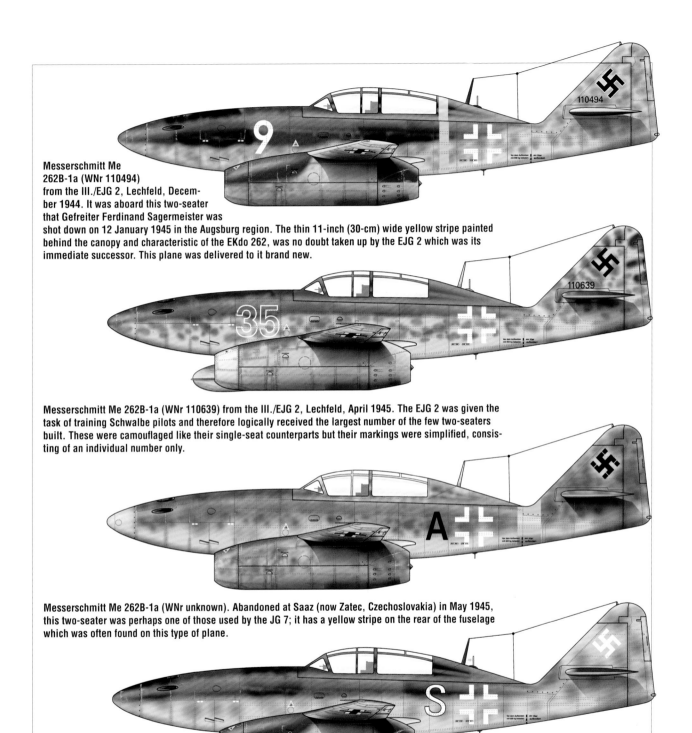

Messerschmitt Me
262B-1a (WNr 110494)
from the III./EJG 2, Lechfeld, December 1944. It was aboard this two-seater
that Gefreiter Ferdinand Sagermeister was
shot down on 12 January 1945 in the Augsburg region. The thin 11-inch (30-cm) wide yellow stripe painted
behind the canopy and characteristic of the EKdo 262, was no doubt taken up by the EJG 2 which was its
immediate successor. This plane was delivered to it brand new.

Messerschmitt Me 262B-1a (WNr 110639) from the III./EJG 2, Lechfeld, April 1945. The EJG 2 was given the
task of training Schwalbe pilots and therefore logically received the largest number of the few two-seaters
built. These were camouflaged like their single-seat counterparts but their markings were simplified, consisting of an individual number only.

Messerschmitt Me 262B-1a (WNr unknown). Abandoned at Saaz (now Zatec, Czechoslovakia) in May 1945,
this two-seater was perhaps one of those used by the JG 7; it has a yellow stripe on the rear of the fuselage
which was often found on this type of plane.

Messerschmitt Me 262B-1a (WNr unknown) from the JV 44, Munich-Riem, April 1945. A former III./EJG 2 plane, this two-seater was the
only one of its kind to be used by this short-lived elite unit.

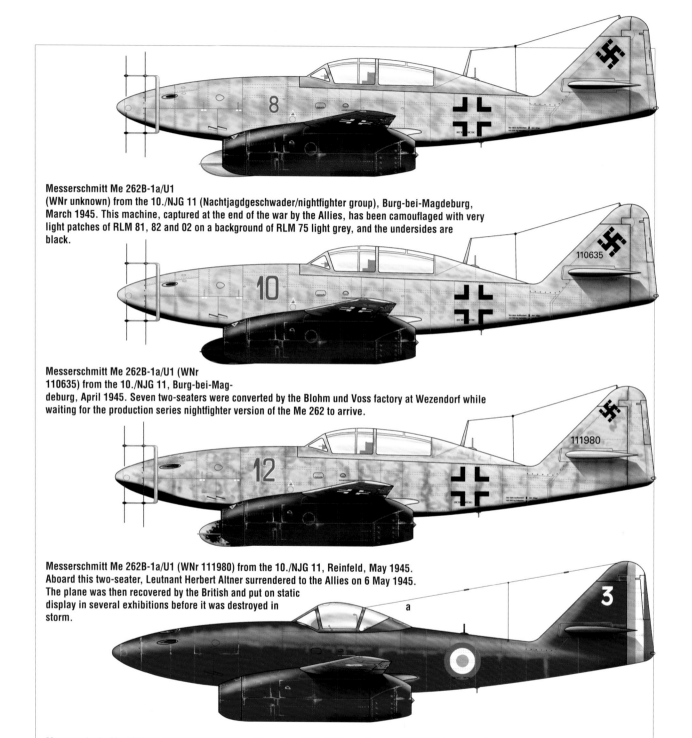

Messerschmitt Me 262B-1a/U1
(WNr unknown) from the 10./NJG 11 (Nachtjagdgeschwader/nightfighter group), Burg-bei-Magdeburg, March 1945. This machine, captured at the end of the war by the Allies, has been camouflaged with very light patches of RLM 81, 82 and 02 on a background of RLM 75 light grey, and the undersides are black.

Messerschmitt Me 262B-1a/U1 (WNr 110635) from the 10./NJG 11, Burg-bei-Magdeburg, April 1945. Seven two-seaters were converted by the Blohm und Voss factory at Wezendorf while waiting for the production series nightfighter version of the Me 262 to arrive.

Messerschmitt Me 262B-1a/U1 (WNr 111980) from the 10./NJG 11, Reinfeld, May 1945. Aboard this two-seater, Leutnant Herbert Altner surrendered to the Allies on 6 May 1945. The plane was then recovered by the British and put on static display in several exhibitions before it was destroyed in storm.

Messerschmitt Me 262A-1a from the CEV (Centre d'Essais en Vol), Brétigny, France, 1948. Put back into flying condition at the SNCASO, this plane made its first flight at Brétigny on 25 March 1947. In all, France recovered eight Me 262s, including a two-seater; most of them were wrecks, and only three were flight tested. This "White 3", the only one painted dark green (the other two were grey) was flight-tested by Armée de l'Air and Navy pilots until a belly landing put an end to its career and the plane, considered beyond repair, subsequently scrapped.

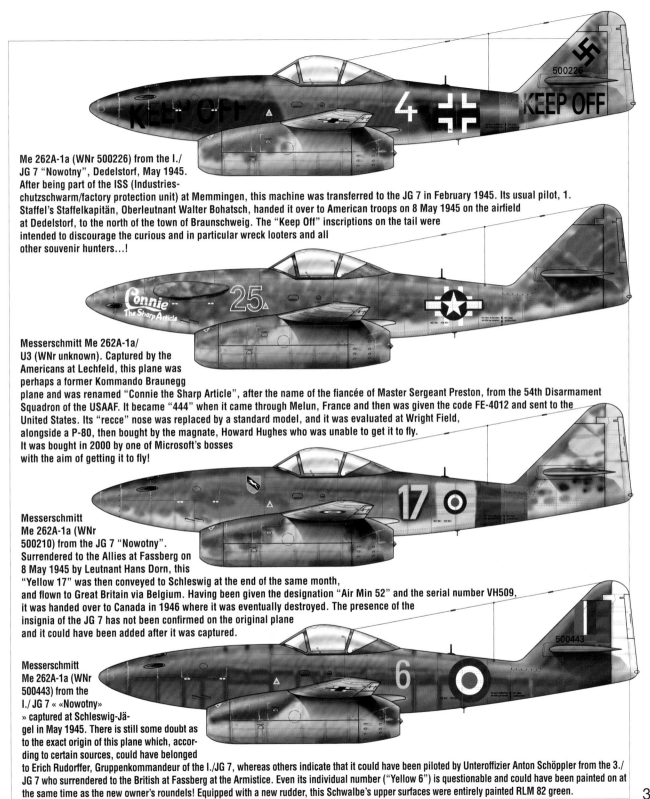

Me 262A-1a (WNr 500226) from the I./
JG 7 "Nowotny", Dedelstorf, May 1945.
After being part of the ISS (Industries-
chutzschwarm/factory protection unit) at Memmingen, this machine was transferred to the JG 7 in February 1945. Its usual pilot, 1.
Staffel's Staffelkapitän, Oberleutnant Walter Bohatsch, handed it over to American troops on 8 May 1945 on the airfield
at Dedelstorf, to the north of the town of Braunschweig. The "Keep Off" inscriptions on the tail were
intended to discourage the curious and in particular wreck looters and all
other souvenir hunters…!

Messerschmitt Me 262A-1a/
U3 (WNr unknown). Captured by the
Americans at Lechfeld, this plane was
perhaps a former Kommando Braunegg
plane and was renamed "Connie the Sharp Article", after the name of the fiancée of Master Sergeant Preston, from the 54th Disarmament
Squadron of the USAAF. It became "444" when it came through Melun, France and then was given the code FE-4012 and sent to the
United States. Its "recce" nose was replaced by a standard model, and it was evaluated at Wright Field,
alongside a P-80, then bought by the magnate, Howard Hughes who was unable to get it to fly.
It was bought in 2000 by one of Microsoft's bosses
with the aim of getting it to fly!

Messerschmitt
Me 262A-1a (WNr
500210) from the JG 7 "Nowotny".
Surrendered to the Allies at Fassberg on
8 May 1945 by Leutnant Hans Dorn, this
"Yellow 17" was then conveyed to Schleswig at the end of the same month,
and flown to Great Britain via Belgium. Having been given the designation "Air Min 52" and the serial number VH509,
it was handed over to Canada in 1946 where it was eventually destroyed. The presence of the
insignia of the JG 7 has not been confirmed on the original plane
and it could have been added after it was captured.

Messerschmitt
Me 262A-1a (WNr
500443) from the
I./ JG 7 « «Nowotny»
» captured at Schleswig-Jä-
gel in May 1945. There is still some doubt as
to the exact origin of this plane which, according to certain sources, could have belonged
to Erich Rudorffer, Gruppenkommandeur of the I./JG 7, whereas others indicate that it could have been piloted by Unteroffizier Anton Schöppler from the 3./
JG 7 who surrendered to the British at Fassberg at the Armistice. Even its individual number ("Yellow 6") is questionable and could have been painted on at
the same time as the new owner's roundels! Equipped with a new rudder, this Schwalbe's upper surfaces were entirely painted RLM 82 green.

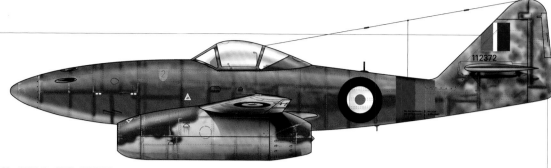

Messerschmitt Me 262A-2a (WNr 112372).
A former 3./JG 7 ("Yellow 17") plane used by the KG(J) 6 ("Gefechtsverband Hogeback") at Prague-Ruzine, this Schwalbe was recovered by the British at Fassberg at the end of the war. It was sent to Farnborough where it was flight-tested in September-October 1945, and it is now on display at the RAF Museum, Hendon, renamed "Yellow 4".

Messerschmitt Me 262A-1a (WNr 111690). This plane from the I/JG 7, built by Messerschmitt at the Schwabisch Hall factory was captured by British troops at Fassberg. Flown to Great Britain with the designation "Air Min 80", it was put on display before being sent to Canada in August 1946. It ended its career as a ground target for shooting exercises in Ontario in 1949.

Avia S.92. The first example of this type, this plane was assembled at the Letnany research institute in 1945 using an airframe in the Avia maintenance workshops, and engines from the Malesice repair workshops, with the Junkers Jumo 004 being renamed M-04. 3. "PL-01", painted greenish light grey (a shade close to the German RLM 02) and decorated with a red lightning flash on the front, made its first flight on 27 September 1946, with the chief test pilot, Antonin Kraus, at the controls.

Avia S-92 from the 5. Stihaci Letka (5th Fighter Group) of the Ceskoslovenské Vojenské Letectvo (Czechoslovak Air Force), end of the 1950s. Czechoslovakia had five "Turbinas" (the Me 262's name that country) including this one, which had retained its original German number (V-33).

MESSERSCHMITT ME 262 CAMOUFLAGE

— Generalities.

In theory, the various parts making up a plane made by the different sub-contractors were painted greenish grey, RLM 02, essentially to stop corrosion since a lot of these parts were made of steel and not of Duralumin. In practice, certain parts, or even the whole plane, were left bare with only the joins covered with Spachtel (primer). The machines, including the prototypes, came off the assembly lines painted entirely pale grey (RLM 76) and were then camouflaged which was often carried out at unit level. Some Me 262 tails, built by the same sub-contractor and fitted to machines delivered to the Kommando Nowotny had been given patches made with stencils and therefore each plane had the same scheme.

— Aircraft from the beginning of the production series (June-November 1944).

The first production series machines were painted according to a scheme similar to that of the Bf 110s, Me 210s and 410s, with large patches and sharp angles of RLM 74 and 75 grey on the upper surfaces, with RLM 76 pale grey underneath. The limit between the patches could be clear or blurred, depending on the aircraft.

— New camouflage scheme.

From September 1944 onwards, new camouflage colours were officially introduced into the Luftwaffe. The Me 262 kept their RLM 76 grey lower surfaces but the upper surfaces were now officially painted RLM 81 and 82. A lot of variations were to be encountered (a single colour on the upper surfaces, extra patches of varying sizes, including the curls) often depending on the machines use (bombers, reconnaissance, etc.); some machines even had a different camouflage scheme on either side of the fuselage, like 9K+IH from the KG(J) 51!

— Nightfighters.

The few two-seat nightfighters built had a camouflage scheme (differing slightly from one machine to another) comprising an RLM 76 light grey background with patches of RLM 75 and/or RLM 75 and 02 of varying shapes and sizes. The wing extrados and the stabilisers also had large patches of RLM 75 an 83 or RLM 82 and 83, whereas the underside was invariably black (RLM 22).

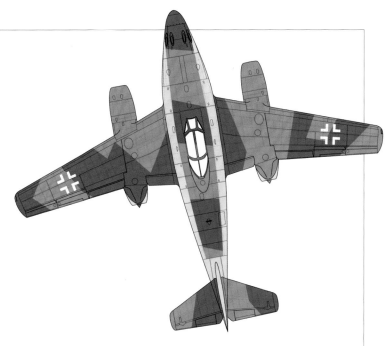

UNIT	CODE	FUSELAGE STRIPE
JG 7	none	red/blue
KG(J)6	none	black/red checkerboard
KG(J) 51	9K	
KG(J) 54	B3	blue/white checkerboard
KG(J) 76	F1	

OFFICIAL COLOURS OF THE GERMAN JETS

RLM 02 Grau (grey-green)
RLM 04 Gelb (yellow)
RLM 21 Weiß (white)
RLM 22 Schwarz (black)
RLM 23 Rot (red)
RLM 24 Dunkelblau (blue)
RLM 27 Gelb (yellow)
RLM 65 Hellblau (light blue)
RLM 70 Schwarzgruün (green-black)
RLM 71 Dunkelgrün (dark green)
RLM 66 Schwarzgrau (grey-black)
RLM 74 Graugrün (grey-green)
RLM 75 Grauviolett (violet-grey)
RLM 76 Lichtblau (light blue)*

RLM 81 Braunviolett (violet-brown)
RLM 82 Hellgrün (light green)
RLM 83 Dunkelgrün (dark green)

Because of a lack of the raw materials needed to make the paints at the end of the war, variants existed for the RLM 76 which could range from the official light grey blue to a greenish grey.

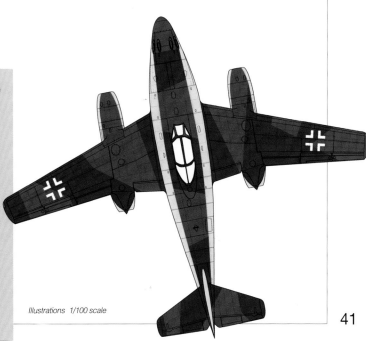

Illustrations 1/100 scale

ARADO AR 234 « BLITZ »

The Arado Ar 234 is noteworthy in the history of flying for two reasons: it was indeed the second jet to enter service officially in the Luftwaffe, but it was also the first mass produced jet bomber put into service in numbers, all in the last year of the World War Two.

This plane was in fact designed just after the war started, at the end of 1940, when the German authorities set up studies for a fast, long-range (1 325 miles/2 150 km) reconnaissance aircraft powered by two jet engines that were being developed at the time both at Junkers and at BMW. At the beginning of 1941, a team led by Walther Blume, the manager of Arado, and Hans Rebeski looked into the matter and put forward various studies, one of which was designated E.370 at first and finally 8-234. It was a high wing monoplane powered by jet engines in underwing nacelles. Its range was to be more than 1 250 miles (2,000km) with a top speed of 500 mph (800 kph) at 19 700 ft (6 000 m) and a maximum ceiling of 33 000 ft (10 000 m). The plane was originally designed around the BMW P.3302 (later 109-003) jet engine but difficulties fine-tuning the engine made Arado modify its project so that it could use other engines like the Junkers Jumo 004 or the Daimler Benz ZTL 5 000.

Changing engines and above all having to give the plane the longest range possible resulted in the fuselage being lengthened to carry more fuel which had a knock-on effect on the type of undercarriage used. A rather unconventional system using a bogie fitted with a series of nine small wheels retracting into the airframe together with skids fitted under the engine nacelles was considered for a time; this was rejected and it was decided that the E-370 would take off using a separate tricycle trolley, controlled by hydraulic brakes while taxiing and equipped with parachutes so that it could be recovered once jettisoned, since the plane landed on three retractable skids, the main ones being installed under the engine nacelles in order to protect them.

Prototypes and first trials

In February 1942, Erhard Milch at the time Head of the Reich Armament, went to the Arado factory at Brandenburg where the E.370 was shown to him. Impressed by the forecasted performance figures of the plane (1 250-mile range and more than 500-mph top speed and a 33 000-feet ceiling), the following April the RLM authorised the production of the plane's first two prototypes, officially designated Arado 234, with a further order for test machines arriving shortly afterwards.

Although the first prototypes (V1 and V2) were built quickly, they couldn't start their trials straightaway because the first pair of jet engines which were to power them – two Jumo 004B-0s – were only delivered a year later, in February 1943 and even then these engines were only intended for static and taxiing tests. At that time Messerschmitt had priority where the supply of jet engines was concerned for its Me 262 and Arado had to be happy with what it got… These engines were supposed to deliver some 1 870 lb (850 kg) thrust each but this figure quickly turned out to be theoretical, so much so that other methods were used to increase power on take off. Being towed by two Heinkel He 111s was considered for a moment but this was abandoned in favour of adding two Walther 109-500 assisted take-off rockets (Rauchergerät).

From the third prototype onwards, all the Ar 234s were equipped with the system for carrying these boosters which worked with a mix of hydrogen peroxide (T-Stoff) and sodium permanganate (Z-Stoff); they each weighed 616 lb (280 kg) giving 1 100 lb (500 kg) of thrust for 30 seconds. Fitted under the outer part of the wing, near the engines, they could be jettisoned after use and recovered since they were fitted with parachutes.

On 18 April 1943, the first Ar 234 (V1) prototype was dismantled and taken by road to Rheine, near Munster where it was given its new engines, this time flight certified and with which they quickly started carrying out ground tests before finally taking off on 30 July 1943 with *Flugkapitän* Selle, Arado's chief test pilot, at the controls.

This flight lasting less than fifteen minutes took place without major mishap except for the take-off trolley which was destroyed because the parachutes which were supposed to bring it back to earth after it was jettisoned failed to open properly. As a similar incident occurred during the second flight on 30 July when the plane had reached a top speed of 406 mph (650 kph), it was decided to jettison the chariot as soon as the plane started lifting off and no longer when it was at a height of only 200 ft (60 m) so that it didn't actually leave the ground and therefore didn't risk getting damaged by returning to earth more brutally than planned.

The V1's career stopped abruptly on 19 August when it had an accident while landing which almost completely destroyed it, rendering it irreparable.

The second prototype (V2)'s maiden flight took place a couple of days later on 13 September and the V3's on the 29th of the same month. This plane was in fact the prototype for the future first production series version, the Ar 234A, fitted with a pressurised cockpit, an ejector seat and rocket assisted take-off. Its career ended tragically since Selle was killed on 1 October 1943 when his left hand engine caught fire after going out. Shortly beforehand at the RLM in Berlin, Arado had been asked to make a bomber version of its jet, and two prototypes, designated Ar 234B "Blitz" (lightning, but the nickname "Hecht" – pike – was often given to it) were immediately ordered. Using the chariot turned out to be not really practical since it made landings on the skids a delicate manoeuvre and left the immobilised planes very vulnerable after landing for at least half an hour before the maintenance teams could replace them on their chariots; and above all, because it prevented bombs from being attached under the fuselage and the wings, it was decided to install normal undercarriage on the aircraft which resulted in the fuselage having to be redesigned and widened in order to house the new, narrow track tricycle landing gear with its maximum speed being reduced slightly by 18 mph (30 kph).

Selle's tragic accident in the end had no effect on the programme which was given the highest priority so that in September 1943, four prototypes had already taken to the air: V4 on 26 September, quickly followed by V5 on 22 December equipped with two Jumo 004B-0s each rated at 1 870 lbf (850 kg) and whose take-off chariot had been modified.

Ar 234 V1 on its take-off chariot with the landing skids down, on the

The Ar 234 V1 on its trolley, skids fully spread, on the Arado factory airfield at Brandenburg/Neundorf. This aircraft made its first flight on 30 July, 1943. It wears the standard camouflage for the Luftwaffe bombers, consisting of dark green (RLM 70-71) upper surfaces with a slight splinter pattern and pale blue (RLM 65) undersides .

TECHNICAL SPECIFICATIONS (Ar 234B)

Type

Single-seat bomber

Powerplant

Two Junkers Jumo 004B axial flow jet engines rated at 1 980 lbf (900 kgp)

Dimensions

Wingspan: 47 ft 3 in (14.40 m)

Length: 41 ft 4 in (12.60 m)

Wing area: 284.167 sq ft (26.40 m²)

Height: 14 ft 1 ½ in (4.30 m)

Weight (empty): 11,440 lb (5 200 kg)

Weight (loaded): 20,823 lb (9 465 kg) with two Walter 109-500 rockets and one 1 100-lb (500-kg) bomb

Performances

Max. Speed: 462 mph (740 kph) (clean) or 431 mph (690 kph) with 1 100 lb (500 kg) of bombs at 19 700 ft (6 000m)

Range: 970 mph (1 550 km) with 1 100 lb (500 kg) of bombs.

Armament

Two 20-mm Mauser MG 151/20 cannon with 200 rounds each and firing backwards (apparently never fitted on the production series). 1 100 lb (500 kg) offensive load under the fuselage

Above.

After working for 50 seconds, the HWK 500 rockets were jettisoned and landed by parachute so they could be used again.

Arado factory airfield at Brandenburg-Nundorf. This machine made its first flight on 30 July 1943. It is wearing the standard Luftwaffe bomber camouflage, consisting of sharp-angled green patches (RLM 70 and 71) on the upper surfaces and pale blue (RLM 65) on the undersides.

The following year it was the turn of the first prototype of the future four-engined planes, the V6, powered by four BMW 003A-1s rated at 1 760 lbf (800 kg) each installed in separate nacelles (first flight on 8 April 1944) and the V8 (1 February 1944) which was powered by the same engines but installed in pairs under the wings; this layout was preferred because it was more aerodynamic. As for the V7, the last Ar 234A to fly, on 22 June 1944, it was basically identical to the V5 but had been fitted with two cameras at the rear of the fuselage, and its engines were Jumo 004B-1s each rated at 1 980 lbf (900 kg).

The first Arado 234B prototype and above all the first machine fitted with conventional tricycle undercarriage, the V9, flew for the first time on 10 March 1943, quickly followed by the V10; it was unpressurised and had no ejector seat but it did carry two ETC 503 bomb launchers under the engine nacelles and was used to test bomb aimers. Seven other prototypes were built, intended for various trials, most of them for the engines:

— V11: the third prototype of the Ar 234B, identical to the V9 which flew on the 5 May 1943 and was mainly used for altitude and speed tests.

— V15 and V17: intended for testing the BMW 003A-1 engines which had a lot of restarting problems once they had gone out, even after the gas regulation system had been installed for the Jumo 004.

— V12 and V14: similar to the V10.

and finally the V13: equipped with four BMW 003A-1s installed in nacelles in pairs, a configuration which had already been tried out on the V8.

— In June, in the presence of Erhard Milch, the V10 reached 512.5 mph (820 kph), a performance which impressed the German authorities so much that comparative tests with the Me 262 were ordered, tests which turned out to be so favourable to the Blitz that a series of twenty Ar 234B-0s (coded S1 to S20) was officially ordered with the first of them (S1) flying as early as 8 June 1944.

From pre-production series to combat

The ambitious mass production plans for this plane were very quickly thwarted by the situation over German territory in 1944, subjected as it was to massive, almost daily air raids by the Allies who wanted to disrupt its production. Even though the Arado factories, situated in the East, had only suffered slightly during the "Big Week" in February 1944 which was aimed at German plane factories, the inevitable production reorganisation which resulted considerably slowed down new models coming off the production lines since production was concentrated on existing models.

But now a new element was to play a major role in the Arado 234's career and even give it the opportunity to prove itself: the Allied landings in Normandy on 6 June 1944. The German General Staff had no idea of the exact strategic situation before and after this operation

An Ar 234B-2 from 9./KG 76 taking off from Burg, assisted by Walther HWK rockets which made up for the weak thrust from the Jumo 004s by themselves. *(SHD Air)*

since the Allies ensured they had mastery of the skies over the battle-field with their marauding fighters shooting down any reconnaissance aircraft that ventured over the front. So it was decided to send over the new jet which, because of its high top speed, was the only aircraft type of the period able to carry out this type of mission and break through the enemy defence network (the Me 262, although just as fast, didn't have the range).

Two prototypes (V5 and V7) each equipped with two RB 50/30 ca-meras were therefore brought together in a specially created unit, the Versuchsverband Oberkommando der Luftwaffe (VV OKL) based at Orianenburg, near Berlin and their two pilots, *Oberleutnant* Horst Götz and *Leutnant* Erich Sommer started endurance flight trials at the end of June. On 25 July 1944 the two planes were ordered to go to France, to Juvincourt near Reims, to start their reconnaissance flights. The V5, piloted by Götz, the unit commander, suffered a breakdown during the trip and had to turn around; so only the V7 reached its destination. After being forced to wait there for a week for its take-off chariot and other equipment to arrive, it was only on 2 August and flown by Sommer that the first reconnaissance mission by a jet aircraft in history was carried out. Flying at more than 437 mph (700 kph) at an altitude of more than 29 500 ft (9 000 m), the V7 took an impressive number of photos of the Normandy and Western France beachheads with impunity.

The V5 flown by Götz finally reached its destination for this histo-ric day and for the next three weeks, the two prototypes carried out thirteen recce missions over the combat zones as well as over Great Britain, each time without running into any opposition from the Allies who weren't even aware that they were flying over at very high altitude and at great speeds.

As the airfield at Juvincourt was coming increasingly under threat from the advancing Allies, the two aircraft were moved to Chièvres, Belgium on 27 August. When it reached this airfield, the V5 was da-maged by friendly fire, before being run into on the ground by an Fw 190 which reduced it to a wreck. Sommer, the only survivor, continued his missions before being sent to Volkel in Holland on 30 August and finally to Rheine, near Osnabrück in Germany on 5 September when the prototype's reconnaissance missions ended because the produc-tion series machines, now fitted with conventional undercarriage, were now available to replace them.

Reconnaissance missions

Götz's unit, christened "Kommando Sperling" (the Sparrow detach-ment) quickly took on charge three new pilots and three pre-produc-tion series Ar 234B-0s, and its strength was nine planes now based at Rheine. Until the 1 November, these planes made 24 operational sorties without any of the engine problems that affected the Me 262. Indeed even if the Jumo 004s had to be serviced every ten flying hours and changed after 25 hours only, the men in the Kommando Sperling had been trained to prolong their life cycle as much as possible, avoi-ding in particular abrupt changes in engine revs. During one of these missions the Allies discovered the new machine for the first time, when some P-51 Mustangs from the 339th FG of the USAF escorting some bombers over Holland ran into an Ar 234 which they weren't able to intercept because it was flying higher and faster than them.

The photo missions were generally carried out at an altitude of 29 500 ft (9 000 m) with an interval of 10 to 12 seconds between shots; the cameras had nearly four hundred feet (120 m) of film each. A number of missions were carried out directly over

Great Britain, the plane's speed enabling it to elude enemy planes without any problems.

On 10 November 1944, another Arado 234-equipped unit was created when Oberleutnant Sommer was sent back to Biblis (north of Mannheim) to form the "Sonderkommando Hecht" (the "pike" trial unit), originally equipped with a single plane (T9+EH from the VVOKL). Two

This Ar 234B from 9./KG 76 (F1+MT) was the first example of this type recovered by the Allies. Forced to land by some P-47Ds from the 366th FG, it landed almost intact near Segeldorf and was then examined by the English at Farnborough. Note the original camou-flage covered with uneven light grey patches (RLM 76).

Opposite.
Bombing trials with one of the Arado 234 prototypes. Because it didn't have a bomb bay, the bombs could only be carried under the fuselage or underwing, which greatly reduced the offensive load.

others (T5+EH and T5+HH) arrived on the following 15 January, a few days after its personnel.

The Sonderkommando Hecht was disbanded on 1 February 1945 and changed to the 1(F)./100 (Fernaufklärungsstaffel – long distance recce squadron) whose maximum strength reached ten Ar 234s (of which only four were operational) and eleven pilots at the end of February, figures reduced to eight planes (eight operational) a fortnight later on 14 March when the unit changed base, after carrying out its missions over Remagen, since Biblis had been taken without a fight on 26 March. After moving to Lechfeld on 5 April then to Munich-Reim where several planes were damaged in air raids, 1(F)./100 lost one Ar 234, shot down by a P-51 Mustang on 18 April. After a short stay at Hörsching (Austria) on 3 May, the unit was disbanded on the day of the armistice in Europe, 8 May, when it was on the border between Bavaria and Czechoslovakia.

— 1(F)./123 was created on the orders of the General des Aufklärungsflieger, from the 3(F)./Aufklärungsgruppe (Nacht) which had been deactivated since May 1944, and assigned together with 1(F)./100 to support Army Groups B and G on the Western Front. Based at Rheine and commanded by Götz, it recovered three machines from the Sonderkommando Sperling.

· In January 1945, the Arados from the two West groups hardly flew because of the very bad weather conditions, carrying out missions on the 2, 14, 20 and 24 January only, over the towns of Liège, Bastogne and Antwerp. On the other hand these flights didn't run into any opposition because of the planes' high speeds and it was finally only on 11 February 1945, six months after it was put into service, that one of these two-engined planes was shot down by a Tempest from N°274

Squadron which had been able to take advantage of the only moment when the machine was vulnerable, i.e. during the take-off and landing phase when it had to fly much slower.

In order to carry out reconnaissance missions over Great Britain and in particular the great naval base at Scapa Flow, but also to operate on behalf of the U-Boats sailing in the North and the Baltic Seas, two little units of Ar 234s were set up in Scandinavia:

— 1(F)./5 (planes coded 9V+xx) settled at Stavanger in Norway on 26 February 1945 with a single plane, joined a couple of days later by two more. The first missions from Norway were carried out between 10 and 23 March, the Arados being fitted with drop tanks to increase their range; one of them was lost in an accident on take-off on 23 March. On the 21st April, the 1(F)./5 was disbanded by the General der Aufklärungsflieger (Chief of Staff of Reconnaissance Aircraft Units) and re-designated Einsatzkommando (operational detachment) 1(F)./33.

— 1(F)./33 (8H+xx) was based at Grove in Denmark and started its missions at the beginning of April 1945. At the time of the Armistice, these two units had seven Ar 234s in Norway and six in Denmark.

A last reconnaissance unit was formed in February 1945 at Udine in Italy, called the "Sonderkommando Sommer", after its commanding officer. It was created from the Sonderkommando Götz which had been withdrawn from the front and moved to Udine in Italy on 26 February. It started its first sorties on 19 March. Equipped with three Ar 234B-1s, this detachment used them mainly to reinforce the watch kept on Allied troop movements in the Ancona region until the war ended and suffered no losses during the few months it was active. The Ar 234s in the reconnaissance units fought until the Armistice with about 24 of them being in service in the four groups on 10 April 1945, the last date for which reliable figures are available.

The Arado 234 bombers

The Kampfgeschwader (bomber group) 76, one of the oldest and most prestigious units in the Luftwaffe and at the time equipped with Junkers Ju 88s, was chosen to become the first group to be equipped with Arado 234s. For this it was entirely withdrawn from operations

---

1. First the Stab under the command of Oberst Robert Kowalewski, then the 6. Staffel. On the other hand it is most likely that 7./KG 76 which remained at Burg at least until March 1945 never became operational. As for the I. and III. Gruppen, they started training in January 1945.

The Arado 234 V9, the first example fitted with conventional tricycle landing gear. Note the one-ton "Hermann" bomb under the fuselage and the pylons under the engine nacelles which could take extra bombs or drop tanks.

on 7 June 1944, the day following the Normandy landings and its III. Gruppe (which consisted of Staffeln 7, 8 and 9) sent to the Arado factory at Alt Lönnewitz where it was given the first production series machines. Converting to the new jet had been ordered by Göring in person and was to take place as quickly as possible, with the crews being trained by pilots from KG 76 who had received special instruction at the Rechlin trials centre, and the ground personnel (mechanics, etc.) visiting the production lines and watching the test flights in order to get themselves acquainted with the new technology.

On 1 September 1944, III. Gruppe was sent to Burg near Magdeburg to continue its training and at the end of the month, it had seven available aircraft. Faced with the urgency of the situation it was decided to concentrate at first all the machines in one Staffel since getting the jet bombers operational and training the crews was taking longer than planned (originally twelve weeks); this was because of the large number of modifications made, together with the numerous accidents caused by the lack of practice and knowledge of the pilots who were changing abruptly from piston-engined planes to jets, which were so much faster and more delicate to master. So the 9. Staffel was declared operational by mid-December 1944 with a full strength of twelve Ar 234B-2s[1]. The unit was led by *Hauptmann* Dieter Lukesch, a holder of the Iron Cross with Oak Leaves who had already carried out 370 bombing missions, whilst a lot of the pilots had already carried out more than 100 operational sorties.

On 17 December, the 9. Staffel was sent to Münster-Handorf so as to be able to take part in the Battle of the Bulge (Ardennes) which had started a day earlier. At that time the unit had ten operational machines. Although this move was finished by the 21st, the bad weather over the region at first prevented any operations taking place. As the weather got better three days later, the jet bombers' début took place on the morning of 24 December, with its first ever war mission, involving eight bombers each armed with one 500 kg bomb under the fuselage, all sent against the town of Liège. This sortie was followed by another on the same day involving the same number of planes against the same target with all of the machines returning safe and sound to their base, where six extra Ar 234Bs were delivered in the evening in order to make up their strength.

Two other raids against Liege took place on 25 December during which an Arado was hit by a Tempest from No 80 Squadron RAF but nonetheless managed to return to base. The first loss occurred on 27 December when a pilot was seriously wounded following a take-off accident. Lots of missions were carried out to the end of 1944, sometimes up to sixteen a day when the weather permitted. Each time the technique used was the same, bombing with a slight dive after flying at low altitude (less than 3 200 ft/1 000 m) and high speed in order to avoid the enemy defences.

The first night bombing mission took place on 1 January 1945 when four jets were sent over Belgium and Holland in order to study the weather conditions in preparation for Operation Bodenplatte, the massive attack using almost all the Luftwaffe planes available on the Western front. In order not to reveal the mission's real target, the machines which flew over Rotterdam and Antwerp at high altitude, bombed Liege and Brussels on the way. A second night time mission took place shortly afterwards using six Ar 234Bs which attacked the RAF airfield at Gilze Rijen with AB 500 fragmentation bombs.

All throughout January, bomber activity was very subdued because of the bad weather conditions; moreover the lack of fuel prevented flying except for four days, respectively the 2nd (attacking Liege), the 14th (Bastogne) and the 20th and 24th January (bombing Antwerp). Besides at the time, operational jets in the units were actually particularly rare. So on 10 January 1945 the Luftwaffe General Staff had an inventory made of all the machines in service and only 17 Ar 234Bs out of the 148 off the production lines were actually available (12 in the 9./KG 76, 4 in the Kommando Sperling and one in the Kommando Hecht) with I./KG 76 and the rest of III. Gruppe waiting to be re-equipped.

In order to ensure that basic training was more effective and so reduce the number of accidents which in turn reduced the number of operational machines, III./EKG 1 was formed on 27 January 1945 from IV. (Erg)/KG 76 and received two Messerschmitt Me 262 two-seaters for advanced training. The future Ar 234B pilots carried out their first flights on Arado 96s and Heinkel 111s before going over to the Schwalbe. The training was very much speeded up since after less than 30 minutes with the two-seat jets, they carried out six training flights on the Ar 234 most of which were for learning how to bomb with a jet powered aircraft.

Only during the third week of January 1945 was the whole of III./KG 76 placed under the command of Major Butcher and declared operational with a full complement of Arados. On the 23rd of the same month, eighteen machines from 7. and 8. Staffeln were sent to Achmer, with three of them being shot down by Spitfires when they reached the airfield and two other damaged.

On 8 February the weather had improved and seven jets bombed the suburbs of Brussels and on the 16th a mass attack (16 machines) was made against British troops near Cleves. Five days later on 21 February, the biggest sortie in a single day was made involving in all 37 Ar 234B which were

launched against English positions near Aachen. On the 24th, one of the jets was obliged to make a forced landing by a USAAF P-47, thus becoming the first example of this type to fall into Allied hands almost intact. On 25 February, the "Blitzes" of III. Gruppe carried out eighteen sorties against the same British positions, during which one bomber was damaged by two Tempests which had succeeded in intercepting it, whilst another was shot down by a Mustang from 364th FG killing the pilot. Whilst III./KG 76 was converting to the new plane, one of its Staffeln, 6./KG 76, was declared operational at the end of February and at the beginning of March 1945 the Arado attacks concentrated on the Ludendorff Bridge over the Rhine at Remagen which had been captured intact by the Americans on 7 March. This bridge was the Reich's last natural defence in the West so the Luftwaffe concentrated all its effort against this target which was declared "top priority".

Together with Me 262A-2s armed with one 2 200 lb (1 000 kg) SC 1000 bomb, three Ar 234Bs tried to destroy the Remagen bridge on 9 March, but one was shot down. When a second mission failed on the 11th, the following day a different tactic was used. This time it involved 18 sorties with planes equipped with Egon radar-operated aiming systems working

Opposite.
Maintenance scene in the hangars of the III./KG 76. The Jumo engines were always the Ar 234's Achilles' heel their life cycle being only ten hours which in the end was increased to twenty-five explaining why the aircraft were not always available in any reliable way. *(SHD Air)*

Apart from two machines handed over by the British, the United States also tested two Ar 234s given to the US Navy at Patuxent River, including this one (WNr 140148) nicknamed "Jane I" and used by II./KG 76. (USN)

automatically and dropping the bombs on a horizontal course. The bridge was once again bombed on the 13th (nineteen bombers) and 14 March (eleven, four of which where shot down by the increasingly ever-present Allied fighters due to the very clear skies), each time unsuccessfully.

Weakened by these unending attacks but also by the demolition charges which had been placed against it, the bridge finally collapsed on 17 March and KG 76 resumed its missions against a variety of Allied targets in Belgium and in Holland. During one of these missions the first and only "kill" by a jet aircraft against another occurred when an Arado 234 destroyed a Gloster Meteor from No 616 Squadron on the airfield at Melsbroek, near Brussels by bombing...!

After the Remagen attacks, the III./KG 76 resumed its attacks against ground positions or vehicle concentrations when the weather permitted, but the Allied advances and the systematic bombing of the airfields forced the remaining elements to fall back to areas still under Germans control, especially in Schleswig-Holstein. The number of machines available was now very limited and the missions increasingly few and far between because of the lack of fuel, even though KG 76's operations had been given top priority [2].

On 10 April 1945, the entire group came under the command of the Luftflotte Reich and was given five extra Ar 234s on this occasion. When the missions could take place, they were concentrated over German territory itself and above all over the Berlin area from 18 April onwards, mainly to try and slow down the advance of the Russian armoured troops. The last confirmed operation by this type took place on 3 May 1945 when a single Ar 234B was sent against an enemy convoy.

In the end the achievement of these first jet-powered bombers was rather slender, mainly because there were so few

of them and the small load they could carry [3]. The impact of their attacks was, if not ineffective, at least negligible and it is obvious that these jets had no direct effect on the course of events. Indeed the only area in which they turned out to be effective was aerial reconnaissance. Their activity in this domain in the Ardennes, and especially following the enemy's movements, explained why the German troops advanced so rapidly, surprising the Allies. Finally like all jets of the period, beginning with the Me 262s, the Ar 234s were almost invincible when flying at high altitudes but when they were in the slower flight phases especially landing and taking off, they became perfect targets for the omnipresent Allied fighters mounting an almost permanent guard on the airfields and picking them off when they were near home.

Below.
In August 1945 on the airfield at Sola, Norway, an Ar 234 captured by the British being prepared for a test flight. Note the periscope placed on the top of the forward "bubble" intended to compensate for the lack of visibility rearwards. This machine (Work umber 140493) had been assigned to 1(F)./5.

2. On 10 April 1945, the last date on which more or less reliable information exists, less than forty or so Arado 234s (38 exactly) were in service: two in the Stab KG 76, five in 6./KG 76, five in III./ 76, seven in 1(F)./33, six in 1(F)./100, eight in 1(F)./123, three in the Sonderkommando Sommer and two in the Sonderkommando Bonow. It is interesting to compare these figures with those for the machines delivered just before hostilities ceased, respectively 210 Arado 234Bs and 14 four-engined Ar 234Cs.
3. At the height of their activity, the Ar 234s in III./KG 76 carried out 37 sorties in a single day during which 18 tons of bombs were dropped in all. At the same time the Allied bombers dropped more than twenty times that figure on each of the ten targets chosen daily...

Above, from left to right.
In order to increase the Ar 234's range, various trials were carried out in February and March 1945 at Neuburg with the S8 towing a Schleppgeräte 5041 airborne fuel tank, designed from a converted V1 airframe and taking off using a trolley (to be jettisoned) and carrying 880 gallons (4 000 litres) of fuel fed through a pipe passing along the rigid tow-bar.

Opposite, from top to bottom.
The V9 carrying an SC 1000 "Hermann" 2 200 lb (1 000 kilo) bomb under the fuselage, rarely used as this configuration limited the plane's range.

Under each engine nacelle a pylon could carry either a bomb or, as here, a drop tank.

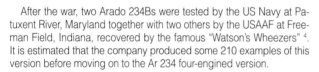

After the war, two Arado 234Bs were tested by the US Navy at Patuxent River, Maryland together with two others by the USAAF at Freeman Field, Indiana, recovered by the famous "Watson's Wheezers" [4]. It is estimated that the company produced some 210 examples of this version before moving on to the Ar 234 four-engined version.

Nightfighter

With Reich territory being raided incessantly by the Allies and particularly at night by the British Bomber Command, the Luftwaffe quickly developed an arm to counter this threat, the Nachtjagdwaffe (the Nightfighter arm). It comprised mainly piston-engined aircraft and when the first jets appeared it was the opportunity to consider using machines which were clearly so superior to their adversaries. As was the case with the Me 262, especially in its two-seat version, an Ar 234 night fighter was also envisaged.

Designated Ar 234B-2/N and nicknamed Nachtigall (Nightingale), this version was equipped with a second cockpit for the radar operator/navigator facing backwards and located on a level with the wing trailing edge where the cameras were housed on the reconnaissance version; it was equipped with a FuG 2218 Neptun V radar whose aerials were placed on the glass bubble the lower half of which was painted black to avoid reflections. Armament comprised two 20-mm cannon in an underbelly gondola. It was planned at first to convert thirty Ar 234Bs into this version, whose prototype (V12) made it first flight on 5 October 1944.

A first Ar 234B-2/N made several operational sorties from Orianenburg, flown by *Hauptmann* Josef Bisping with his radar operator, Hauptmann Albert Vogl, installed in the rear fuselage in a very rudimentary fashion. An experimental unit, the (Sonder)Kommando Bis-

ping, was even created. As Bisping had been killed on 23 February while taking off at night, the mission was taken over by *Hauptmann* Kurt Bonow, formerly an ace with the NJG 5 and 100, in the Sonderkommando Bonow (also called Erprobungskommando 234). This only had three modified machines two of which only were operational. Bonow

4. During the last months of the conflict, the US's Air Technical Intelligence (ATI) entrusted Colonel Harold E. "Hal" Watson with the job of getting hold of the most modern German planes and in particular the jet propelled ones. A small team made up of pilots and mechanics, nicknamed "Watson's Whizzers", after passing through France (after the whistling sound made by the jet engines), got their hands on a rather considerable number of Me 262s, Me 163s, He 162s, Dornier Do 335s and of course several Arado 234s. Most of these planes were flight tested after the Armistice, particularly at Melun-Villaroche in France and the tests continued in the United States where several machine were shipped.

Above.
Front view of the V6, the only prototype equipped with four BMW 003 jet engines installed in separate nacelles. Note the way in which the machine, without conventional undercarriage, has been installed on its take-off chariot. *(DR)*

and his radar operator, *Oberfeldwebel* Beppo Marchetti were quickly joined by two other night fighter aces, *Oberleutnante* Gustav Francsi and Josef Putskühl.

These Ar 234B-2/Ns were mainly used to try and intercept the Mosquitoes, their most deadly adversaries without scoring any kills though, before being lost in accidents respectively on 23 February and 1 March 1945.

The four-engined Ar 234C

After the Versuchsverband Oberkommando der Luftwaffe carried out trials on the four-engined V6, V8 and V13, and after some 200 examples of the two-engined Ar 234Bs had come off the production lines, it was decided to mass-produce this version, called the Ar 234C and powered by four BMW 103A-1s. The first prototype was designated V19 and the second (V20) was fitted with a pressurised cabin.

The production series envisaged – the Ar 234C-1 and C-2 – were in fact only B-1s and B-2s incorporating the improvements made to the V20, with the C-1 being armed with two MG 151/20 firing rearwards in defence. Very few of the first four-engined versions were in fact produced before production was directed towards the "multi-role" Ar 234C-3, of which five prototypes were built (V21 to V25). They featured a redesigned cockpit, heightened to improve visibility, two forward firing cannon installed in a gondola under the nose. When WWII ended on 8 May 1945, only fourteen Arado 234Cs had come off the production lines (a figure to be compared with the 210 Ar 234Bs delivered) and didn't have the time to be assigned to a regular operational unit. ❏

PLANNED VERSIONS, NOT PRODUCED

In February 1945, when the Arado factories were given the job of producing Fw 190s whose production sites had been put out of action by Allied air raids, a lot of projects were purely and simply abandoned, with research concentrating mainly on the Ar 234Cs and Ds.

The main versions of the Ar 234C envisaged

— Ar 234C-3/N: two-seat night fighter armed with two MG 151/20 cannon and two MK 108+s firing forwards and equipped with FuG 218 Neptun and FuG 350 radars.

— Ar 234C-4: reconnaissance, equipped with two cameras and armed with two MG 151/20 cannon.

— Ar 234C-5: side-by-side multi-role two-seater, a configuration tried out on the V28.

— Ar 234C-6: reconnaissance two-seater, tested on the V29 prototype.

— Ar 234C-7: night fighter similar to the C-3/N but a side-by-side two-seater equipped with FuG 245 Bremen radar. All these planes were powered by four BMW 003A-1s.

— Ar 234C-8: single-seater powered by Jumo 004Ds rated each at 2 315 lbf (1 050 kg). At the end of the war, two prototypes (V31 and V40) being built were to have resulted in the single-seat Ar 234D-1 bomber and single-seat night fighter D-2, powered by two HeS 011A-1 engines being developed.

Other projects were still on the drawing board, like the Ar 234E two-engined bomber (two HeS 011A-1s), or the Ar 234F heavy fighter (Zerstörer) or bomber, identical to the D but larger and powered by two Jumo 012s.

Another series was envisaged, the Ar 234P, of which five variants were already envisaged: four two-seat night fighters with different weapons and engines (four BMW 003A-1s on the P-1 and P-2, two HeS 011 or two Junkers 004D on the P-3 and P-4) and a three-seat night fighter, the P-5, powered by a pair of HeS 011s. The last machine planned was the Arado 234R, a recce version powered by a Walter 2-ton-thrust rocket engine which was to have been towed aloft before being launched at 2 600 ft (800) m by a Heinkel He 177a. Research was also carried out on the shape of the wings – crescent-shaped or of composite construction (metal and wood). Some of these configurations were tested on the V16 and V18 prototypes.

Below.
The Arado 234C-3, the four-engined version with engines in tandem in underwing nacelles. About fifteen of these aircraft were produced, none being allocated to a fighting unit, for lack of time. As with the production Ar 234B, the skids were replaced by a conventional tricycle undercarriage.

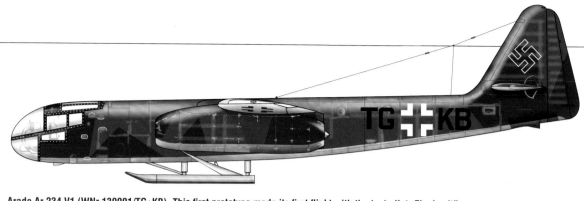

Arado Ar 234 V1 (WNr 130001/TG+KB). This first prototype made its first flight with the test pilot, Flugkapitän Selle, at the controls on 30 July 1943. It was seriously damaged landing at Brandeburg a few days later on 29 August 1943 and never flew again. As with all the prototypes, the conventional undercarriage was replaced by skids (one ventral and two lateral), take off being done using a little trolley which was jettisoned once the aircraft was airborne.

Arado Ar 234 V7 (WNr 130007/T9+MH). This plane, the first to be powered by Jumo 004B turbojets made its first flight at Alt-Lonnewitz on 22 June 1944. It was sent to France with the V5 in July 1944 and was given the tactical code T9+MH, becoming the first jet plane to carry out a reconnaissance mission when on 2 August 1944, it flew over the landing beaches in Normandy, supplying the Germans with information on the state of the front which Allied air superiority had denied them ever since 6 June 1944.

Arado Ar 234 S10 (WNr 140110/E2+20) from the Erprobungskommando 234, Rechlin-Lärz, November 1944. This plane was the pre-production series example and was used to try out the FuG 203 radio guidance systems for the Henschel Hs 293 antishipping missile.

Arado Ar 234B-2 (WNr 140113/F1+AA) from the Stab (HQ) of the KG 76. Achmer, March 1945. Used by Oberstleutnant Robert Kowalewski, this Blitz was captured by the British on Schleswig airfield at the end of the war and sent to England. According to a KG 76 habit, the front ring of the air intakes was painted the Staffel's distinctive colour—here green, attributed to the Geschwaderstab—which is to be found again on the individual letter of the registration ("A").

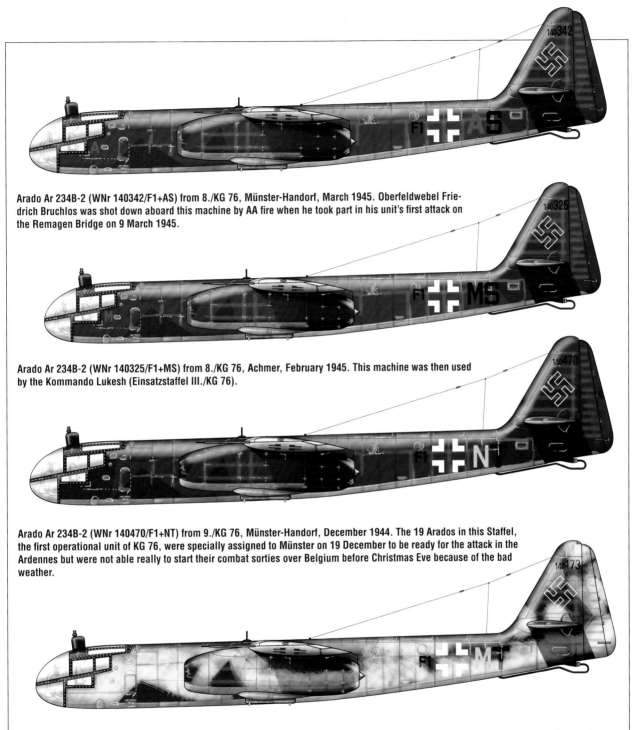

Arado Ar 234B-2 (WNr 140342/F1+AS) from 8./KG 76, Münster-Handorf, March 1945. Oberfeldwebel Friedrich Bruchlos was shot down aboard this machine by AA fire when he took part in his unit's first attack on the Remagen Bridge on 9 March 1945.

Arado Ar 234B-2 (WNr 140325/F1+MS) from 8./KG 76, Achmer, February 1945. This machine was then used by the Kommando Lukesh (Einsatzstaffel III./KG 76).

Arado Ar 234B-2 (WNr 140470/F1+NT) from 9./KG 76, Münster-Handorf, December 1944. The 19 Arados in this Staffel, the first operational unit of KG 76, were specially assigned to Münster on 19 December to be ready for the attack in the Ardennes but were not able really to start their combat sorties over Belgium before Christmas Eve because of the bad weather.

Arado Ar 234B-2 (WNr 140173/F1+MT) from 9./KG 76, Münster-Handorf, February 1945. The personal mount of the 9./KG 76's "Staka", Hauptmann Josef Regler, this Arado made a belly landing near Segelsdorf on 22 February 1945, after being damaged by USAAF P-47s. This was the first aircraft of this kind recovered by the Allies and was quickly sent to Farnborough, UK to be carefully examined. Apart from its winter camouflage, note the individual letter the same colour as that of the Staffel, on the top of the fin.

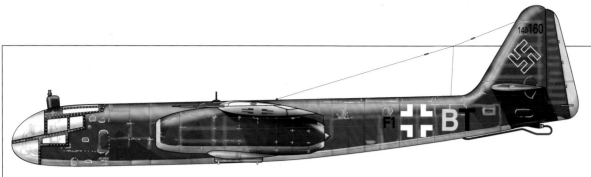

Arado Ar 234B-2 (WNr 140160/F1+BT) from 9./KG 76. Münster-Hansdorf, December 1944. This plane was piloted by Leutnant Diether Lukesch, appointed Einsatzerprobungskommando Ar 234's CO in October 1944, then promoted to Hauptmann (captain), he was put at the head of 9./KG 76 from December 1944 to the end of February 1945. Then as Kommandeur, Lukesh commanded the III./Erg. KG 1, then the IV./KG 76. When he surrendered to American troops with his unit, he was credited with 430 combat missions, five kills and the destruction of 12 oil tankers. After the war he became a civilian pilot and ended his career as flight captain aboard a Boeing 707!

Arado Ar 234B-2 (WNr 140151/T9+KH) from the Kommando Sperling (whose insignia can be seen under the left glass panel showing a farting sparrow…). Rheine, end of 1944. This machine was used by Oberleutnant Werner Muffey who was transferred from the Kommando Götz to the Kommando Sperling in February 1945, where he was Technical Officer before joining the 1.(F)/123 in April 1945. The Kommando Sperling was created at Rheine with recce Ar 234Bs and personnel from 1./Versuchs-kommando OKL. Disbanded in January 1945, it was absorbed by 1.(F)/100.

Arado Ar 234B-2b (WNr 140341/9V+AH) from the Einsatzkommando of the 1./ Fernaufklärungsgruppe 5 (FAGr. 5). This machine made a forced landing on 23 March 1945, its pilot, Leutnant Helmut Hetz, being wounded. Formed in January 1945 at Quakenbrück, this unit was renamed Einsatzkommando 1./FAGr.1. in May 1945.

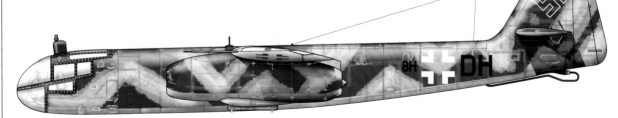

Arado Ar 234 (WNr 140476/8H+DH) from the 1./Fernaufklärungsgruppe 33 (1./FAGr 33 or 1.(F)/33—33rd Long Range Reconnaissance Group), Jüterborg-Waldlager, Germany, February 1945. In order to make the plane less visible the original camouflage on the upper surfaces (RLM 81, 82) has been covered with irregular white or light grey patches (perhaps RLM 76) .

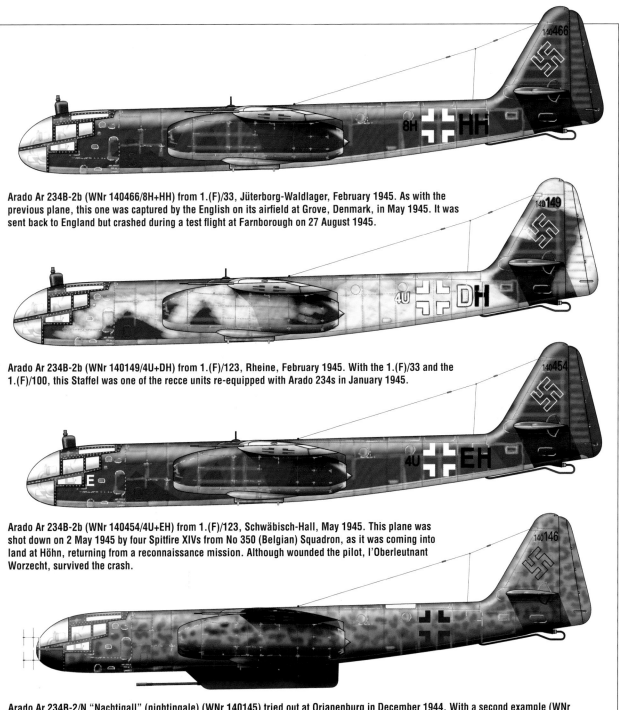

Arado Ar 234B-2b (WNr 140466/8H+HH) from 1.(F)/33, Jüterborg-Waldlager, February 1945. As with the previous plane, this one was captured by the English on its airfield at Grove, Denmark, in May 1945. It was sent back to England but crashed during a test flight at Farnborough on 27 August 1945.

Arado Ar 234B-2b (WNr 140149/4U+DH) from 1.(F)/123, Rheine, February 1945. With the 1.(F)/33 and the 1.(F)/100, this Staffel was one of the recce units re-equipped with Arado 234s in January 1945.

Arado Ar 234B-2b (WNr 140454/4U+EH) from 1.(F)/123, Schwäbisch-Hall, May 1945. This plane was shot down on 2 May 1945 by four Spitfire XIVs from No 350 (Belgian) Squadron, as it was coming into land at Höhn, returning from a reconnaissance mission. Although wounded the pilot, l'Oberleutnant Worzecht, survived the crash.

Arado Ar 234B-2/N "Nachtigall" (nightingale) (WNr 140145) tried out at Orianenburg in December 1944. With a second example (WNr 140146), this plane formed the Kommando Bonow, then Kommando Bisping when Bonow was killed. This is an interim version of the nightfighter while waiting for the Ar 234C-3/N production series model. Its armament comprised two 20 mm MG 151-20 cannon installed in a Magirus bomb converted into a ventral nacelle; it is also equipped with a FuG 218 Neptun wide-band pursuit radar and a FuG 350 Naxos radar detector. The operator was installed in the rear part of the fuselage facing backwards where the cameras were usually fitted on the single-seat version.

MESSERSCHMITT ME 163

The Messerschmitt Me 163 Komet also has a special place in aviation history as it is still, even today, the only rocket-powered interceptor to have been mass-produced and used in combat, scoring several confirmed kills.

The story of this strange aircraft goes back to the first half of the 20th Century and more particularly to the work of the German engineers, Alexander Martin Lippisch and Gottlieb Espenlaub, influenced by the ideas of Friedrich Wenk on tail-less delta-wing gliders (flying wings). When Lippisch joined the Rhön Rositten Gesellschaft (or RRG) in 1925 in Wasserkupe, specialising in glider research, he designed four prototypes between 1921 and 1926 giving them the name *Storch* (stork) I to IV.

In 1933, Lippisch joined the DFS *(Deutscher Forschungsanstalt für Segelflug* – German glider research institute) in Darmstadt-Griesheim, created on the Nazi Party's initiative secretly to recreate an air force, banned at the time by the Versailles Treaty. Appointed head of the technical department at DFS where he remained until 1939, Lippisch wasn't very successful since the RLM forbade him to continue research on tail-less gliders after two accidents had occurred with two such aircraft. However, the manager of DFS, Professor W. Georgii, who was convinced of the basic soundness of the engineer's research, managed to get this decision rescinded and even offered him a post in his institute.

Lippisch's very first design for DFS was the Storch IX, a tail-less glider like the first Storchs whose development had been stopped when the engineer turned his attention to the delta wing formula. This project was followed by the Delta IV which spurred three successive variants (Deltas IVa, b and c) of which the last had a less pronounced sweptback wing and two fins added to the wing tips. Powered by a 75 bhp propeller engine, the Delta IVc was sent to the test centre at Rechlin in 1936 where it was officially given the designation DFS 39. Finally in 1938 the DFS 40 (Delta V) appeared, a real unpowered flying wing with a cockpit sunk into the forward part of the wing which made its maiden flight still with

Above.
This Me 163B (WNr 191659 "Yellow 15") was captured intact at Husum in May 1945 and sent to Great Britain. It joined the collections of the East Fortune Air Museum, Scotland in 1976.

Opposite.
Delta 1 in flight in 1931: the basic shape foreshadows the future Komet.

Opposite.

The DFS 194 being built and taking off. Although the general design foreshadowed the Komet, there were a number of differences both on the tail and the cockpit canopy. On this prototype, the engine was housed inside the airframe which did not make modifications or replacements easy.

Heinrich "Heini" Dittmar at the controls in 1939. This "two-seat sports plane" obtained its airworthiness certificate and an improved second example was ordered by the RLM as part of the specifications for a tail-less, pusher-engined fighter project, using the simple name of Entwurf X (project X). This new prototype, officially designated 8-194 and DFS 194 by Lippisch and his team working secretly in Darmstadt, was to be equipped with a "special engine", an HWK R-I-203 rocket motor [1]. When the advanced research was finished in the AVA wind tunnel in Göttingen, Lippisch noted that the fins placed on the wing tips, like on the DFS 39, caused heavy vibrations and that a conventional central tailfin was needed, with the rudder giving the tail better control. Right from the start the DFS 194 had a central belly skid replacing conventional undercarriage, take off being done by means of a two-wheeled chariot which was jettisoned once the aircraft was airborne.

For practical reasons and for a question of available space, the prototype, now known simply as "Projekt X", was built, half by DFS for the wings and by Heinkel for the fuselage. As sharing the work turned out to be disastrous with no progress being made at all, at the beginning of January 1939, the RLM transferred Lippisch to Messerschmitt at Augsburg where, in the greatest secrecy, he formed Abteilung L (Section L—L for Lippisch) with 12 engineers as well as Heinrich Dittmar.

---

1. HWK for Helmut Walter Kiel Kommandogessellschaft. The R-I-103 worked by mixing T-Stoff (T-fuel, highly corrosive and made up of 80% hydrogen peroxide with oxyquinoline or sodium phosphate added as a stabiliser) and Z-Stoff (an aqueous solution of calcium or potassium permanganate) serving as a catalyzer and transforming the oxygen peroxide into steam. The operating temperature at the exhaust outlet was around 500°C. This type of engine was so-called "cold".
2. Ever since 1936, Heinkel had been working, at first officially then at his own expense, on a jet aircraft, the He 176, equipped with the same Walter rocket engine, but which only flew for the first time in June 1939. It was particularly disappointing as far as performance was concerned and the machine caused so much scepticism among the authorities that developing it was finally forbidden in September the same year…

In this new set up, the researcher, now benefiting from much more freedom as well as more means, decided to break away from the conventional combustion engine and carry on with the rocket.

With his team Lippisch made a demonstrator with the rebuilt DFS 194, using mainly wood in place of aluminium and using the power from a Walter HWK R-I-203, identical to the one used by the He 176 [2], but whose thrust had been reduced to 660 lbf (300 kg). The DFS 194 was finished in early 1939, and engine trials began at Karslhagen, the airfield at the Peenemünde test centre, on the Baltic coast, the following October. When war began in September 1939, the programme was delayed a lot but the DFS 194 reached Peenemünde in February 1940. It was tested there first as a glider, towed up by a Bf

The first Me 163 prototype (V4) made its first unpowered flight in February 1941 but only received its engine six months later. Like all the prototypes of the rocket fighter, including "Bertha", it was painted glossy light grey (RLM 76) all over with black code letters.

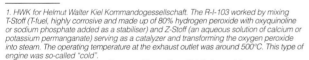

TECHNICAL SPECIFICATIONS Me 163B (Me 163A)

Type
Single-seat interceptor

Powerplant
One Helmuth Walter Kiel Komman-dogesellschaft HWK 109-509B rocket motor with variable thrust, rated at 220 lbf to 3 300 lbf (100 to 1 500 kgp)/ 109-509A motor rated at 330 lbf to 1 650 lbf (150 to 750 kgp)

Dimensions
Wingspan: 30 ft 6 in/29 ft (9,30 m/8,85 m)
Length: 18 10 in/17 ft 2 in (5.75 m/5.25 m)
Wing area: 210.976 sq ft/188.368 sq ft (19.60 m²/17.50 m²)
Height: 8 ft 2 in/7 ft (2.50 m/2.16 m)
Weight (empty): 3 300 lb/2 530 lb

(1 500 kg/1 150 kg)
Max. take-off weight: 8 580 lb/4 840 lb (3 900 kg/2 200 kg)

Performance
Max. speed authorised 594 mph (531 mph)/ 950 kph (850 kph)
Operational ceiling: 39,300 ft (12 000 m)
Max. engine endurance: 7 minutes
Rate of climb: 2' 27" at 19,700 ft (6 000 m). 2'84" at 26,250 ft (8 000 m). 3' 24" at 32,800 ft (10 000 m).

Armament
Two 20-mm Mauser MG 151/20 machine guns fitted in the wing roots replaced after the 47th example with two 30-mm 60-round Rheinmetall Borsig MK 108 cannon.

110, with ballast used to simulate the engine and fuel tanks weight. The powered first flight took place on 3 June 1940 with Dittmar at the controls and during the subsequent trials it turned out to be far superior to the He 176.

A speed of 345 mph (550 kph) in level flight was indeed reached during one of the last test flights whereas a limit of 187 mph (300 kph) had been decided on originally and the machine showed it could reach an astonishing climb rate of 5 300 feet (1 615 metres) per minute during the very short lapse of time (150 secs) that the engine functioned.

From "Anton" to "Bertha"

Despite the failure of the He 176 and the doubts it raised among the RLM officials, all of this in wartime conditions where the new industrial priorities had placed development of jet engines well in the background, the DFS 194's success caused renewed interest in the concept so much so that at the start of 1941, the official green light was given for Messerschmitt to make two prototypes intended for development purposes, designated at first Lippisch P 01 V1 (V for *Versuchsträger*, research example), and V2, then very shortly afterwards Me 163A V4 and V5 [3].

The two prototypes were ready at the end of the winter of 1940-41 and basically resembled the DFS 194 with only one tail, a larger rudder, more sweep to the wing leading edges and a rounder cross-section to the fuselage. As for the automatic leading edge slats, they had been replaced by slots situated directly at the wingtips, a feature that was maintained on all the Me 163 production series machines. The HWK R-II-203 (109-509A according to the RLM designation) rocket engine used by these two prototypes used a mix of two chemicals, Z-Stoff (calcium permanganate) and T-Stoff (hydrogen peroxide) producing thrust which could be regulated between 330 and 1 650 lbf (150 and 750 kgp).

The Me 163 V4 (KE+SW) flew for the first time without an engine, at Lechfeld, an airfield situated near Augsburg, on 13 February 1941. During a series of gliding flights which were carried out afterwards, the plane, towed aloft by a Bf 110, reached more than 531.25 mph (850 kph) in a dive, without an engine, remember. The prototype was sent to Peenemünde in June-July 1941 where, after being equipped with its Walter rocket, it made its first powered flight on 10 August

The Me 163B V8, one of the first ones to have received vents at the exhaust nozzle to avoid the until then recurring problems of extinction of the rocket motor. Note the deployed skid and faired tail-wheel in landing configuration. The aircraft is entirely RLM 76 glossy light grey.

1941 (13th according to some sources). After quickly beating the world speed record (471.87 mph/755 kph), a few weeks later, on 2 October, during its fourth powered flight, it reached a speed of 627.29 mph (1 003.67 kph) or Mach 0.84, in a dive after being towed up to 13,120 feet (4 000 m) by a Bf 110 to save as much fuel as possible and increase its range, a record which was only beaten six years later, after the war, by the famous "Chuck" Yeager, aboard the Bell X-1. The pilot could no doubt have gone beyond that speed if he hadn't been confronted with compression problems on the wing tips at the approach of what wasn't yet called the speed of sound and forced to cut the engine prematurely to avoid losing lift and going into an uncontrollable dive.

Dittmar's historic flight, which remained a secret because of the war, so impressed the Head of the Luftwaffe, Reichsmarschall Göring, that he wanted to be kept informed of the programme's developments. As for Ernst Udet, the *Generalluftzeugmeister* (the director-general of aviation equipment), he ratified Messerschmitt's proposal to have the company Wolfgang Hirth Werke build eight pre-production models designated Me 163A-0 ("Anton") intended for trials and pilot qualification, followed by four prototypes of the Me 163B (V1 to V4) together with an airframe for structural tests carried out by Messerschmitt in his Augsburg factory. These machines were followed by another order for 66 [4] production series machines built in the Regensburg-Obertraubling factory.

Installing the engine and the armament was to be done by Klemm in its Stuttgart-Böblingen factory, which was also given the job of making the plane when the Regensburg site was switched to Bf 109 only production at the end of 1943.

The Me 163B, or Bertha, differed from its predecessor by the constant sweep of its wings, a larger redesigned fuselage (metal instead of wood as on the Anton), a pointed, armoured nose-cone, a redesigned canopy without frames, a fairing housing a retractable skid and tail wheel, and finally more fuel capacity.

At the beginning of 1942, Udet's replacement, Erhard Milch, had Hauptmann Wolfgang Späte brought back from the Eastern Front

where he was CO of the 5./JG 54 and appointed him Typenbegleiter (coordinator) of the Me 163, with the job of organising the programme, from the factories making the motors and the airframes to setting up a training unit, the idea being to get the fighter into service as quickly as possible and to sort out all the various problems.

Unfortunately the company, Walter, was having so much difficulty producing the R-II-203 rocket motor, that only four examples were available at the time at Peenemunde. As a result the second prototype (V-5, code GG+EA), which had flown for the first time without an engine on 8 November 1941, could only make its first powered flight at Peenemunde on 29 April of the following year.

The initial, unrealistic, delivery schedules for the rocket fighters were modified several times, with the programme being delayed many times, mainly because supplies were lacking. The prototypes only left the factory in April 1942, but without any actual information about the engines, the HWK R-II-209s originally planned being replaced by R-II-211s, which meant modifying the position of the fuel tanks and therefore further delays.

The Me 163B V1 (code VD+EK) was equipped with the Anton's so-called "cold" engine, the HWK R-II-203 (109-509A), which also equipped the B V4, V6 and V8, and started non-powered flights on 26 May 1942. The definitive model of the engine, the R-II-211 (109-509B) "hot" using a mix of C-Stoff and T-Stoff was fitted to the other prototypes except the B V10 and V 14, kept aside for the future BMW engines.

The Bertha programme was modified several times in the course of 1942 and 1943, mainly due to the delays with the trials, the recurrent

---

3. It was given this designation in order to keep the programme "top secret" and to deceive the enemy although a small two-seat light plane, the unlucky rival to the Fieseler Fi 156 Storch, had already been given the name in 1938. The deception was taken even further as the first prototype of the "new" Me 163, was the V4 and not the V1, in order to keep up the fictitious series started with the two-seater. According to the German radio alphabet, the Me 163A was called "Anton" and the B "Bertha".
4. As a general rule and despite all period documents confirming it, this batch has been divided by most authors into 40 pre-production series Me 163B-0s armed with 20-mm MG 151/20 whose barrels protruded from the wing leading edges, and 30 production series B-1s equipped with 30-mm MK 108s sunk entirely into the wings.

lack of mechanics assigned to the project and because of the priority given to the Me 262. After producing an initial batch of Komets (up to V 22), Messerschmitt passed on the production of the following examples to Klemm, with assembly suffering further delays due to additional modifications on the planes, in particular installing extra armour, radio equipment and above all changing the on-board armament, the original 20-mm machine guns being replaced by 30-mm cannon after the B V45. In January 1945, all the B-0s and half the B-1s had come off the assembly lines but they were only gradually fitted with their powerplants during of the following month. Engine production had been slow despite relentless, round the clock work in the Walter factory at Kiel. About half the pre-production series B-0s were held on to by Messerschmitt for trials and the other half were delivered to the *Erpobungskommando* (EKdo) 16, a special trials unit whose first task was to test the rocket engines, which the engine builder had not been able to do as he hadn't had the time nor the fuel.

Technical description

The Me 163B, the production series Komet, was a single-seat, tailless, mid-wing aircraft. The plane's construction was mixed so that production could be sub-contracted out as much as possible, thereby reducing the risks of supplies being interrupted in the case of a production unit being bombed. The fuselage was semi-monocoque and oval, covered in aluminium with flushed rivets. The central caisson was semi-circular and had fairings covering the join between the wings and the canopy and the belly. The wings were made up of a double spar covered with plywood and bolted to the fuselages with ferrules. The wings were swept back at a constant angle of 23.3° to 25% of cord; there was a fixed slot on the leading edge intended to

prevent stalling. The moving surfaces were a pair of lift-increasing flaps and two elevons (elevator-ailerons functioning individually) fabric covered and equipped with large trimming tabs.

The tail consisted of a fin with a rudder but no horizontal surfaces. The forward point of the fuselage was armoured and was equipped with a small propeller activating a generator to supply the electricity needed by the very modest on-board avionics, consisting of FuG 25a and FuG 16zy radios. The cockpit was located in front of the fuel tanks which, together with the engine, took up almost all the space in the fuselage; there was no ejector seat and the cockpit was protected by a one-piece acrylic plastic windshield opening to the right; inside there was a 90-mm thick armoured windshield.

On the first pre-production series examples, armament consisted of two 20-mm machine guns recognisable by their barrels sticking out of the wing leading edge; these were replaced by a pair of 80-round 30-mm Rheinmetall Borsig MK 108 cannon located on either side of the fuselage in the wing roots. As an experiment one Me 163A-0 was given 24 57-mm air-to-air Orkan rockets whilst a dozen production series Berthas were equipped with ten 50-mm recoil-less Lanweiler SG 500 Jägerfausts on the wing tips.

For reasons of space and weight, the conventional undercarriage was replaced by a two-wheeled trolley, jettisoned once the aircraft was airborne, at precisely 16 ft (5 m) so as to avoid any rebound which could damage the aircraft, and a retractable steering tailwheel. The aircraft landed at very high speeds (more than 136 mph/220 kph) on a retractable skid under the fuselage whose shock absorber had a very short life cycle, as trials and operational use were amply to demonstrate. This system was the cause of a great number of accidents (80%), so many that fitting a tricycle undercarriage was very seriously envisaged for the machine's later versions (Me 163C/263).

The Me 163B was powered by a liquid fuel Walter HWK 509 A-2 (the official designation of the R-II-211) rocket motor rated at 3 520 lbf (1 600 kgp); the fuel consisted of 490 litres of C-Stoff, carried in unprotected tanks set in the central part of the wings, and of 1 160 litres of oxidant, the T-Stoff, housed in the fuselage tanks (behind and on either side of the cockpit). Various attempts were made to improve this rocket engine, especially in the form of the 109-509C motor with variable thrust up to 2 tons and equipped with an extra chamber giving 440 lbf (200 kg) fixed thrust, for less consumption and increased flying time. Series production of the 109-509C motor, intended for the future Me 163C with a longer, pressurised fuselage, was ready in February 1945 but only a few pre-production series examples were available before the end of hostilities, which were nonetheless tested on prototypes V6 and V18, enabling the latter to reach the unbelievable (for the times) speed of 706 mph (1 130 kph) in flight.

To take off the Me 163 was towed to its take-off point where the mechanics set the starter. A steam turbine system of two centrifugal pumps pressurised the two fuels into the combustion chamber and triggered an immediate explosion, giving the thrust needed for take off. The machine climbed at a rate of almost 300 ft/sec (90 m/sec)

at an angle of between 50° and 80°, which enabled it to reach an altitude of some 29 500 ft (9 000 metres) in a little more than two and a half minutes, and its operational ceiling of 39 370 ft (12 000 m) in 3 minutes and 20 seconds. It had a range varying between 2 ½ to 8 minutes depending on how the engine was working and the pilot's skill, with the plane being guided from the ground towards the enemy formation nearly twenty miles away.

A typical mission consisted of climbing to just below the height of the bombers, between 22,900 ft (7 000m) and 29,500 ft (9 000 m), slowing the engine and continuing to climb on its own momentum. The pilot had to be careful levelling out to avoid the engine going out, since restarting the engine took at least two minutes and used up at least 660 lb (300 kg) of fuel. He then attacked the target from behind and at the same height, even though a frontal attack was possible against a bomber. Once this single fly past on a near-collision course over, the Komet's pilot climbed again on its momentum until it ran out of fuel; he could then carry out another attack, this time gliding down from above. As the Komet's attack speed was very high, nearly 500 mph (800 kph), there was little chance of it being hit by the bombers' defensive fire but its own chances of hitting one of them were also very meagre since the target was only in the Komet's sights for three seconds at most, and the cannon's rate of fire was too low, as was the ammunition's muzzle velocity

The plane glided back to base with a draining system making sure that not a drop of fuel was left in the tanks, the slightest contact in them causing a catastrophic explosion. Once the engine had gone out, the Me 163 returned to being a glider and could reach 700 kph in a dive, with the landing taking place after a steep dive at a speed of 131-156 mph (210-250 kph) on a airfield where a cross showed the pilot where to place the central skid. The Komet landed in 390 to 760 yards (360-700 m) depending on how damp the ground was.

The difficult beginnings in EKdo 16

Formed on 20 April 1942, the EKdo 16's main tasks were to train future pilots and to outline how to use the new fighter operationally (specific training for mechanics, preparing interception procedures, working with the ground stations, etc.) Logically, the unit was placed under the command of Wolgang Späte who carried out the first powered flight aboard Me 163A V4 on the following 11 May, seconded by Rudolf "Rüdi" Opitz.

The flight tests were carried out for a while by a small group of specialists including Heinrich Dittmar (who had already flown the DFS 39 and 94, as well as the V4), Joachim Pöhs, Johannes Kiel and the famous Hanna Reitsch, a authority on gliding in which she had competed before the war. In fact, she was one of the numerous victims of the Komet's particularly demanding character when on 30 August 1942, during an unpowered flight aboard Me 163A V5, its undercarriage refused to jettison despite her efforts. She tried to crash land but ended up in an accident in which she hit the sights installed in the cockpit for the trials with her face and was seriously wounded. Before being taken to hospital she insisted on doing her professional duty and drew up her flight report then passed out! After five months in hospital and plastic surgery, she resumed Me 163 flight trials but

her former colleague, Wolfgang Späte, thought she'd done more than enough for the mission and had her quickly leave the team.

In November 1942, the EKdo 16's strength comprised several Antons and five Berthas (V1 to V5) and development of the plane continued during the winter of 1942-43, even though flights had been rendered impossible by the bad weather conditions.

After they arrived, the pilots started training aboard two-seat DFS Kranich and Granau Baby gliders before being let loose on the Habicht acrobatic gliders, some of which had had their wings shortened. The pupils then carried out unpowered flight aboard an Anton towed up by a Bf 110 before making their first powered flight with this version and finally converting to the Bertha.

As the Peenemunde centre had been bombed during the night of 17/18 August 1943, the EKdo 16 was forced to move to Bad Zwischenahn, near Oldenburg with its seven Me 163As and single Bertha. Shortly after this move, twenty or so pilots arrived at the new base in order to constitute the first operational unit. These men were in turn confronted with the interceptor's particularly susceptible and demanding character whose design together with the quite unusual powerplant (very brutal start-ups and cavitation problems in the fuel tanks causing the engine to cut out inopportunely) needed not only a solid experience but also a good dose of good luck.

which ran on a mix of SV-Stoff (nitric acid) and M-Stoff (methanol), resulting in thrust of between 660 lb (300 kg) to 3 300 lb (1 500 kg). But problems encountered in getting the fuel injection pumps to work properly delayed this engine's production so much that it was never operational before the end of the war.

The pupils' first flights began in January 1944 when the EKdo's 16 personnel consisted of more than 500 men but all flights had to be cut short the following month because of bad weather conditions in the region and because there were a lot of enemy fighters around as soon as the skies cleared. The unit had nine operational Berthas at the end of February, but only one in a fit state to fly, so it was able to start its operational training, simulating interceptions.

The Komet's first combat mission—and at the same time, the first by a propeller-less plane – took place on 14 May 1944 when Späte, aboard Me 163B V41 (code PK+QL) painted entirely red as a tribute to the Fokker Dr1 of the legendary WWI ace, Baron von Richtofen, tried to intercept a group of US planes heading for Bremen and which had been picked up on the Wurzburg Riese radar screens at Bad Zwischenahn. His engine had gone out when he suddenly spotted two P-47s flying above him; he managed to restart it after the necessary 2-minute time lapse and headed towards them. As he neared 565 mph (900 kph), his left wing suffered from the effects of compressibility and stalled; the engine went out a second time, forcing Späte to abandon his attack. After trying a second interception on the same day, he left for the Eastern Front and was replaced at the head of the training unit by Hauptmann "Toni" Thaler.

Several missions took place during the following days (on 19 May with *Oberfeldwebel* Nelte aboard B V40 or 22 May with Rudolf Opitz aboard B V33), each time unsuccessfully because the pilots were unable to spot their targets. This activity ended up by drawing the Allies' attention, and they bombed Bad Zwischenahn on 30 May 1944, destroying at least one machine (V33) completely and damaging five others, together with the gliders and the Bf 110 tug. Activity at the base was disrupted until 15 June, with the EKdo 16 being sent temporarily to Brieg-an-der-Oder where no flights took place.

The EKdo 16 Komets then started to be camouflaged and given a fuselage code beginning "C1" specially attributed to the unit.

After another large-scale air raid on 15 August, the unit, with now only six out of fifteen planes, was finally transferred to Brandis, near Leipzig at the start of October 1944, where it remained until it was disbanded in February 1945. Apart from its original mission, developing the Me 163, the EKdo 16 was also given the task of testing its designated successor, the Me 263, of which four prototypes had been officially ordered and which in the end, because they were built by Junkers, were renamed Junkers 248.

At the end of November 1943, sixteen pilots had converted to the *"Kraftei"* (the motorised egg, the name given to the Me 163 by its pilots because of its shape, seen from the side) and the first fatal accident occurred on the 30th of the same month when a pilot was killed aboard B V6 after making a mistake.

But it was the rocket engine and in particular its fuel which was the reason for the many often fatal accidents which did not involve just beginners, proof of the engine's particularly unpredictable character and the trouble getting it to work. Josef "Joschi" Pöhs was killed in a particularly awful manner on 30 December 1943. His machine was damaged by the trolley which had bounced up off the ground immediately after take off; the engine went out and the fuel circuit cut off. With the speed the plane had reached, Pöhs managed nonetheless to reach a height of some 300 feet and veered off to start an approach with the wind behind him. But during this manoeuvre, the Komet ran into a radio mast, crashed and slid along the ground for more than 50 yards. When the rescue teams got to the machine a few moments later, nothing was to be found of the pilot. He had been literally dissolved by the fuel which had splashed all over the cockpit…

There was a slight improvement when a new version of the rocket motor, the Walter 109-509A-2, was installed. It started up less brutally and was fitted with air vents to avoid cavitation problems, and thrust was increased to 3 740 lb (1 700 kg). BMW also had the job of making another motor which could be installed in the Me 163B, the 109-510,

In service with the JG 400

Meanwhile at Bad Zwischenahn in February 1944, the 20./JG 1 was formed and equipped with Me 163s for which ten or so pilots started their training with the EKdo 16. Renamed the 1./KG 400 on 1 March, the Staffel was sent to Wittmundhafen under the command of Hauptmann Herbert Olejnik where its first pilots began arriving a few days later. At the end of the same month it had six Me 163Bs: the fighters were delivered by air, towed from Bad Zwischenahn.

After going through a few powered take-offs, the Staffel quickly began its flight tests, especially for weapons. On the other hand, headquarters had forbidden any operational combat sorties, the planes and personnel having to hide when enemy aircraft were detected in the region in order to preserve the secret as to the very existence of the rocket powered fighter.

Olejnik was wounded on 21 April after making an emergency landing aboard V16 and was replaced as "Staka" *(Staffelkapitän)* by Hauptmann Otto Böhner. The first production series Me 163 reached Wittmundhafen in mid-May 1944 and a few weeks later, when the 1./JG 400 had sixteen fighters, an official demonstration took place with the B V29 and 54 on 12 and 13 June in the presence of several senior officers from the Jägerstab (fighter HQ), Göring himself and Ehrard Milch, accompanied on this occasion by delegations from Italy and Japan, both countries being interested in this aircraft.

The first combat missions were finally allowed in July 1944 without any result and the 1./JG 400 was transferred during July to Brandis near Leipzig, with the planes once again towed there in flight. There they were to protect the synthetic fuel production complex at Leuna, 30 or so miles to the southwest of Leipzig. Deploying the fighter in this way was in complete contradiction to its initial conception. Indeed at first, the plan was to create a network of Me 163 bases[5], 90 miles apart (the plane's maximum range) positioned along the Belgian and Danish borders, and on the approaches to Berlin. From these the interceptors could attack the enemy bomber waves en route to or coming back from their targets. One of the people responsible for changing this strategy was the Komet's new Typenbegleiter, Oberst

Gordon Gollob, appointed by the General der Jagdflieger, the famous Adolf Galland, who replaced Späte when he left for the Eastern Front. Gollob now decided to concentrate the Me 163s near priority objectives in order to protect them.

Brandis was a secondary airfield and not very suitable for the rocket-plane, as it was small and above had little in the way of buildings, especially for storing the dangerous rocket engine propellants. What is more, Leuna, which the JG 400 was supposed to protect, was situated at the very limit of the fighters' interception range, leaving them only a narrow margin of action. Moreover, once installed on this base, the Komets remained there until the end of the conflict.

The three weeks following the Staffel's arrival on its new base were the ones in the Komet's (short) career in which the most important fighting took place. The 1./JG 400's first operational sortie took place on 19 July 1944 when Uffz Kurt Schiebeler unsuccessfully tried to intercept a P-38 aboard B V50 (PK+QU) but ran out of fuel. A few days later, the first reports of encounters with the new machine were drawn up first by RAF pilots then by USAAF pilots, which noted its remarkable performances, particularly when climbing.

A first kill was even claimed on 29 July by a Lightning from 479th FG, a claim which is not confirmed by the German archives.

At full strength at Brandis at the beginning of August 1944 with 16 Komets (four of which only were operational), the 1./JG 400 scored its first kill at the beginning of the same month but on an uncertain date, when *Leutnant* Hartmut Ryll managed to shoot down a B-17. The same pilot was killed several days later on 16 August when he was shot down by escorting P-51s just after scoring his second kill against another Flying Fortress.

During the same mission another Komet pilot was wounded by fire from the bombers but managed to bail out, and Feldwebel Siegfried

---

5. *Wittmundhafen, Udetfeld, Stargard, Deelen, Husum and Venlo had been chosen by the Luftwaffe.*

Schubert managed to shoot down another B-17 with only three 30-mm shells fired at its tail.

24 August was the most successful day since this time four *"Dicke Autos"* (heavy cars, the nickname given Allied heavy bombers by German fighter pilots) were shot down, two B-17s (from the 92nd and 457th BGs) by Schubert and one each by *Leutnant* Hans Bott and *Oberfeldwebel* Straznicky, during a second sortie. *Uffizier* Schiebeler, who had taken part in the Komet's unsuccessful first combat sortie in August, was much luckier on 11 September when he shot down a B-17 in the immediate environs of Brandis, before scoring his second kill the next day over Merseburg.

After this eighth kill, and despite a larger number of Me 163s coming off the production line, the rocket-plane's activities were considerably lessened and its sorties increasingly rare, mainly due to a chronic lack of fuel because the Kiel factory specialising in its production had been literally razed to the ground in an air raid in August. This fuel couldn't even be taken to Brandis by train since the Allies were constantly attacking the German railroad network; then when it did reach its destination, it had to be destroyed because it had been stored too long and had become unusable...

The Me 163s scored no further kills before the end of the year, with bad weather conditions very often putting off any flying. Because of its limited range and because of the way it glided in to land, the Me 163 could only be used in good weather (it is one of the rare machines never to have been used at night), and for its pilot to return to base without any help [6] he could only rely on himself and on landmarks on the ground which had to be perfectly visible in excellent weather conditions.

Worse still, when flying was possible it was accidents, very often dramatic ones, which punctuated the missions. On 7 October, twenty Komets were launched against bombers once more attacking the Leuna refinery, but only two scored hits. During this mission, *Feldwebel* Schubert, the Me 163 top scorer, died when his machine (B V61)

exploded as he was beginning to take off, whereas *Uffizier* Eisenmann was killed when landing.

A second Staffel, the 2./JG 400, was created at Bad Zwischenahn in April 1944. and transferred to Venlo in Holland in the following July where it received its first fighters at the end of the same month. The pilots had trained during the preceding weeks so the first combat mission (again unsuccessful) took place in the middle of August. On 6 September, transporting its planes by road with the wings removed, the 2./JG 400 moved to Brandis after its Venlo installations were destroyed because of the arrival of Allies which was thought to be imminent... but which only took place at the end in March 1945!

A support squadron, the Ergänzungsgruppe (Erg) JG 400, was also created in July 1944 using elements from EKdo 16 and placed under the command of Oberleutnant Franz Medicus. It was given six Komets (Antons V 10, V11 and V13, and the Berthas V1, V4 and V8) of which only V10 was equipped with a rocket motor and its role was to train the pilots. It was also transferred to Brandis in July 1944, and renamed the 13./EJG 2 in November when it was sent to Udetfeld and its tasks shared with the 14./EJG 2 set up at Sprottau.

On 8 September 1944, Major Späte was officially appointed I./JG 400's *Gruppenkommandeur* and Galland declared the Komet operational (incidentally this name, given on an unknown date, appeared only twice, in an official document dating from the beginning of 1945). He was replaced by *Hauptmann* Opitz and the last sizeable engagement took place on 2 November during which three pilots lost their lives: Straznicky, shot down in the Leipzig area; Horst Rolly killed when his plane caught fire on take off; and *Oberfeldwebel* Jakob Bollenrath, shot down by a P-51.

A purely administrative reorganisation of the JG 400 took place on 12 November 1944: the 3. and 4. Staffeln becoming respectively 5. and 6. This reorganisation concluded with the creation of a 7. Staffel and a Stab (HQ) and was intended to set up the II./JG 400 based at Stargard-Klützow, commanded by R. Opitz, with the job of defending the Pölitz hydro-electrical complex, situated within range of the Komets. The I./JG 400 remained at Brandis, but its 4. Staffel, although planned, never materialised.

Just before the end of the year, on 27 December, Späte was appointed the JG 400's Geschwaderkommodore, whose I. and II. Gruppe were placed under the command of Hauptmanns Fulda and Opitz. A third Gruppe, the III./JG 400 was also formed at Udetfeld from the Erg. JG 400 and its 7., 8. and 9. Staffeln were sent to Bad-Zwischenahn, Wittmundhafen and Hordholz respectively on 1 March.

The first weeks of 1945 were marked by an increasing lack of fuel which, together with bad weather, virtually grounded all aircraft. On the 7 March however, a recce Spitfire was attacked by a pair of Komets, but managed to get away from them by diving abruptly, a manoeuvre which had the British pilot going over 500 mph (800 kph).

---

6. At the beginning of October 1944, the CO of I./JG 400, Hauptmann Fuda wrote to tell Gollob that the Komet pilots needed assistance on the ground and a guidance system at least as good as that used for the night-fighters, but for daytime flights.

Opposite.
Rudolf Opitz settling into a Bertha at Bad Zwischenahn. The Me 163 pilot's uniforms, completed by gloves, were made of "Asbestos Mipolamfibre", a non-organic material close to nylon also used for parachutes. The propeller of the generator in the forward tip of the fuselage and the armoured windshield (90 mm) are clearly visible here.

Opposite.
The Me 263, renamed Junkers 248 when that firm was given the job of building it, was to take over from the Komet, production of which stopped in February 1945. It was bigger and fitted with tricycle undercarriage; it would have been easier to fly although not much more effective. Two prototypes only were made in the end making a few unpowered flights before the end of the war.

On 16 March, *Oberleutnant* Rolf Glogner intercepted a Mosquito PR XVI from No 544 Squadron and damaged it without however shooting it down since the twin engined plane succeeded in dragging itself to Lille where it belly-landed.

In April 1945, II. Gruppe which had been forced to move to Husum in Schleswig-Holstein because of the advancing British troops, was up to strength on its base but could not make any sorties because it didn't have any fuel. When it finally got some, flights started again enabling the Komets to score their last official kill on 10 April when *Leutnant* Friedrich "Fritz" Kelb who was part of a group of three Me 163s launched against British bombers, shot down an RCAF Lancaster in the Leipzig region with a Jägerfaust (literally hunting fist) which his plane was equipped with. This quite original system consisted of five 50-mm mortar tubes installed vertically on each wingtip and firing a salvo of rockets using selenium photo-electric cells and triggered by the shadow of the bomber under which the Komet was passing. To perfect this system a rather radical method was used: an Me 163 had to fly at great speed at ground level under some canvas stretched between two posts a bomber's length apart.

At the time it was envisaged converting the I./JG 400 to the Horten Ho 229 flying wing. This unit and its Stab (HQ) were disbanded at Brandis on 14 April and its Komets destroyed to escape capture, since the airfield was taken two days later by the Allies. Späte was sent to JG7 with his four best Komet pilots, including Kelb who was to shoot down a B-17 aboard an Me 262, and thus becoming the only pilot to score kills using two different jets. On 6 May, the II./JG 400 whose CO, R. Opitz was in hospital because of an accident a few days earlier, surrendered to RAF Regiment elements who had captured the base at Husum. Most of the 48 Komets which were recovered by the British came from there and 25 of them were sent to Farnborough and four others supplied to France.

The Me 163's operational balance sheet is quite derisory when you think of the means used to get it operational, but also because of its high cost in human lives. Apart from the fact that the effectiveness of the Komet against the thousands of machines bombing Reich terri-

tory daily was rather like a mosquito sting on an elephant, the ten or so kills scored (just before the surrender of the II. Gruppe, with *Leutnant* Gerth shooting down a Mosquito, unconfirmed) by this rather unconventional fighter were done so at the very high price of fifteen pilots killed, most of them in accidents.

A comet in the land of the rising sun

Warned by its military attachés in Germany of the Me 163's existence, Japan which was also looking for an effective weapon to counter the USAAF's heavy bombers, and in particular the B-29s which flew far too high for its usual interceptors, acquired the rights at the end of 1943 to build the HWK 109-509A under licence. The contract agreed with the Germans stipulated also that an Me 163 in flying condition would be supplied in exchange for strategic materials for the Reich. In the 19-Shi specifications established the following July and concerning an experimental rocket-powered defensive fighter, Mitsubishi was given the job of making the plane and the Yokosuka Navy Air Arsenal *(Daï-Ichi Kaïgun Koku Gijitsusho)* the Toku Ro.2 engine, a copy of the Walter rated at 3 300 lbf (1 500 kgp). The first submarine taking the Komet to Japan was sunk on the way and only an engine reached its destination aboard another, so it was decided in the absence of any real plans, to copy the German fighter using just the instruction manual.

In July 1944 Mitsubishi started making the plane, called Shusui (sabre blow) and designated J8M1 by the Imperial Navy, and Ki-200 by the Army. After a scale one model was presented in September, both arms gave their permission to build several prototypes, and production of a wooden glider the same size was also launched.

Below.
A Bertha from JG 400 at Brandis starting up. The white plume of smoke under the plane was caused by the steam turbine driving the centrifugal pumps which mixed the two fuels.

Above.
The Soviets recovered a few examples of the two-seat glider version of the Me 163S, intended originally for converting future Komet pilots. In December 1944, twelve production series Me 163Bs were sent to the Lufthansa workshops at Berlin-Staaken to be modified. At least six Me 163Ss were produced of which three were assigned to EJG 2 and one to EKdo 16 in February 1945.

Designated MXY8 Akigusa (autumn grass) and intended for training future pilots, three examples of this glider were built by the Yokosuka Arsenal, with its first flight taking place on 8 December 1944. A larger version of this glider was built subsequently equipped with water tanks reproducing the real plane's characteristics, with the machines for the Navy being built by the Maeda Aviation Institute, and the Army's (Ku-13) by the Yokoï Company. Although the exact number produced is not known, it is thought that between fifty and sixty of these "heavy" gliders were produced.

The first two J8M1s, with their engines replaced by ballast, started flying in January 1945 but only six months later, on 7 July 1945, did the Shusui's first powered flight finally take place on the Yokosuka airfield. This ended just as briefly as tragically when just after take off, at less than 1 300 ft (400 m), the engine stopped abruptly, most likely because of a fuel supply problem, causing the plane to crash killing the pilot, Lieutenant Toyohiko Inuzuka. No other test flight took place before hostilities ended a few weeks later and out of the thousand J8M1s and 2s (on the latter a fuel tank replaced one of the two cannon) planned only seven were indeed completed, but no Ki-200s or Ki-202s (with increased range) were produced for the Imperial Army. ❏

PLANNED VERSIONS OF THE ME 163

If prototypes and pre-production series machines are counted (Me 163A-0s and 163Bs V7 to V70, of which eleven examples were destroyed when the Regensburg factory was bombed) together with Me 163B production series machines in 1944 (327 examples) and 1945 (37), 438 examples of the Komet were built in all. On top of those, other versions and variants were also envisaged, most of them never built:

Me 163S: two-seat glider intended for training future Komet pilots (20 examples planned, at least six in fact converted)

Me 163B V6 and V18: two examples fitted with a Walter HWK 109-509C-1 rated at 4 400 lbf (2 000 kgp) and an entirely retractable tail wheel. According to certain sources, the V18 reached 706 mph (1 130 kph) at 16,400 ft (5 000m) on 6 July 1944 apparently.

Me 163C-1: a production series machines fitted with a Walter HWK 109-509-C-1; longer fuselage, teardrop canopy and increased range. Three prototypes were built (V1 to V3) at the end of 1944 but were finally destroyed to avoid them falling onto Soviet hands.

Me 163D: researched at the same time as the Me 163C and equipped with retractable tricycle landing gear. This project was given to a Junkers team with the designation Ju 248 and was dropped in favour of the Me 263; the only prototype built (V1) in August was tried out in the following September and captured by the Allies.

Above.
The MXY8 Akigusa glider intended for training future Shusui pilots in the Imperial Navy. The plane has been painted entirely in orange.

Opposite.
One of the J8M1s recovered intact after the war by the Americans. Unlike its German counterpart, this fighter only made one powered flight which ended in tragedy…

Messerschmitt Me 163B V21 (WNr 16310030) from the Erprobungskommando (EKdo) 16, Peenemunde-West, June 1943. Painted entirely RLM 76 light grey, like all the prototypes, this Komet made its first powered flight on 20 July 1943 and was damaged the following year when the Bad-Zwischenahn airfield was bombed in May 1944.

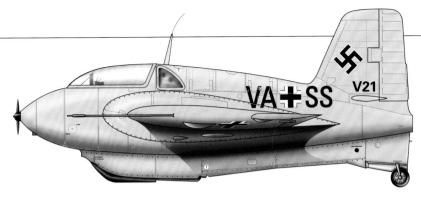

Messerschmitt Me 163B V 35 (WNr 16310044) from the EKdo 16, Brandis, October 1944. This Komet is often shown with a dark coloured rudder but in fact this was because on the pictures of the plane taken when landing the rudder was turned away, the resulting shadow giving the impression that the colour of the rudder was different from the rest of the camouflage.

Messerschmitt Me 163B V41 (WNr 16310060) from the EKdo 16, Bad Zwischenahn, May 1944. For its first operational sortie on 14 May 1944, this Komet, flown by Hauptmann Wolfgang Späte, was painted all red (RLM 23) in memory of Baron Manfred von Richtofen's famous red Fokker Dr. I triplane.

Messerschmitt Me 163B V61 (WNr 16310070) from the 1/JG 400, Brandis, October 1944. There is some doubt about the exact code of this machine which was perhaps GN+ND. It was destroyed on 7 October 1944 when its rocket engine exploded just as its pilot, Feldwebel Siegfried Schubert, was starting off on his second combat sortie of the day.

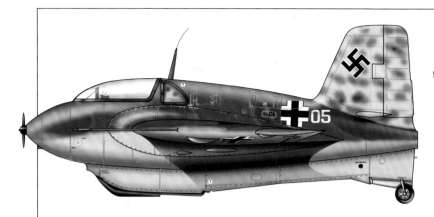

Messerschmitt Me 163B V45 (WNr 16310054/ C1+05) from the EKdo 16, Bad Zwischenhahn, July 1944. Previously coded PK+QP, this Komet, photographed as a wreck after the war, was one of the three Me 163s equipped with the "Jägerfaust". Damaged on 24 December 1944 while testing this spectacular weapon, it made its last flight on 8 April 1945, with Fliegeringenieur Harold Kuhn at the controls. It was at the end of August 1944 that the EKdo 16 planes were given a new camouflage scheme as well as a new identification number, made up of the code "C1", attributed to the unit and painted in very small black letters, in front of the fuselage cross, followed by a white individual number which was much bigger.

Messerschmitt Me 163 V53 (WNr 16310062) from the 1./JG 400, Brandis, August 1944. The first Komets, like this one, used by Unteruffizier Kurt Schiebeler and seen from rear right three quarters profile on a period photograph, had the three-shade of grey (RLM 74, 75 and 76) camouflage scheme still being used by the Jagdwaffe at that time. At the end of its operational career, the "Kraftei", the egg with an engine (the nickname its pilots gave the Me 163) was assigned to the 14./JG 400 (14./EJG 2), the unit with the job of training the pilots.

Messerschmitt Me 163B (WNr 198599) from the 1./JG 400, Brandis, October 1944. The insignia painted on the front is the 1./JG 400's and shows a jet-powered flea climbing, together with the sentence "Wie ein Floh, aber Oho!" (like a flea, but oho!). The nose has been painted white, the 1. Staffel's colour, just like the individual number.

Messerschmitt Me 163B Komet (WNr 191454) from the 6./JG 400, Nordholz, March 1945. Captured at Husum, where the unit was stationed in the middle of April 1945, this Komet was sent to the RAE (Royal Aircraft Establishment) then put on show in Hyde Park, London in September 1945. Handed over to Canada in 1946, it was apparently scrapped at Arnprior, Ontario in 1957.

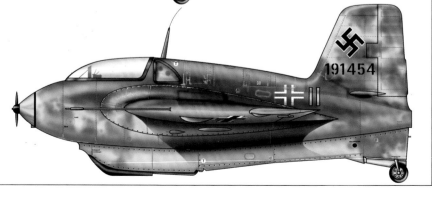

Messerschmitt Me 163B (WNr 440186) in the 1./ JG 400, Bad Zwischenahn, January 1944. The first example made by Klemm Teknik, this machine is visible on a photograph together with an "Anton" (Me 163A) shortly after it arrived at Bad Zwischenahn. Coded TP+TN, "white 8" was assigned to 1./JG 400, and was shot down in the Siester region on 2 November 1944, and its pilot, Oberfeldwebel Herbert Steaznicky, was killed.

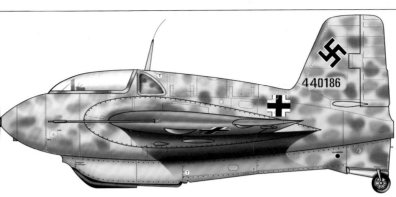

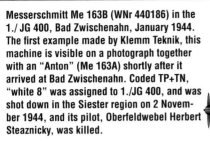

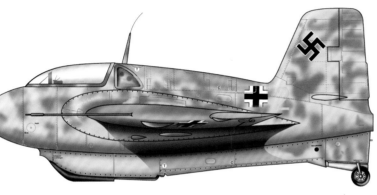

Messerschmitt Me 163B from the 7./JG 400. Photographed at Husum just after the Armistice, there is no information about this Komet which bears the old camouflage scheme with a grey background. The front of the fuselage cone and the individual number was painted yellow, II./JG 400's distinctive colour.

Messerschmitt Me 163B from the 1./JG 400, Brandis, August 1945. Aboard this machine, Unteruffizier Kurt Schiebeler made one of the Komet's first combat sorties (in the end without result) on 24 August 1944.

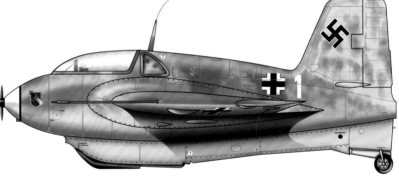

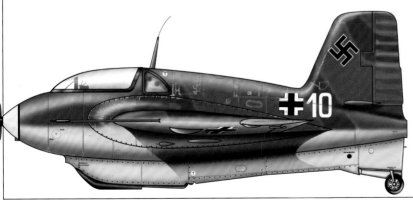

Messerschmitt Me 163B (WNr 190598) from the 1./JG 400, Brandis, February 1945. This Komet, which was part of the first batch built by Junkers, made test flights at Brandis on 20 and 22 February 1945, flown by Leutnant Hans-Ludwig Löscher. Its fuselage is camouflaged with large patches of RLM 81 and 82, but with no speckling, especially on the tail.

69

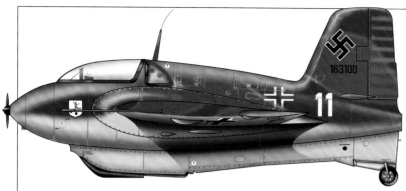

Messerschmitt Me 163B (WNr 163100?) from the 1./JG 400, Brandis, August 1944. Aboard this machine, whose Werk Nummer is not known with any certainty since the official documents make no mention of it, Leutnant Hartmuth Ryll obtained the Komet's first kill, in August 1944 before being shot down himself on 18 August by USAAF P-51 Mustangs escorting some bombers, thus earning for himself the sad privilege of being the first KG 400 pilot to be killed. The insignia painted on the front is the JG 400's showing the famous Baron of Munchausen, riding on his cannonball.

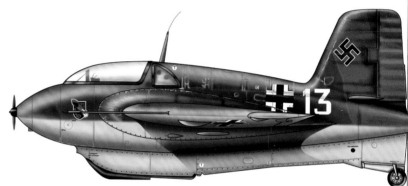

Messerschmitt Me 163B (WNr unknown) from the 1./JG 400. Although it appeared in a period film, there is no information about this plane which bears the 1./JG 400 insignia.

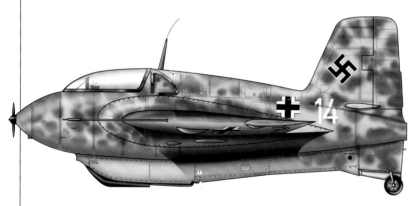

Messerschmitt Me 163B (WNr unknown) from the 1./JG 400, Brandis, August 1944. The period photographs bear witness to the presence of two "white 14" at Brandis and Witmundhafen, distinguished by their camouflage, this one having, unusually, a fuselage speckled with RLM 81 and 82, whereas it was usually only the tail which was speckled in this way.

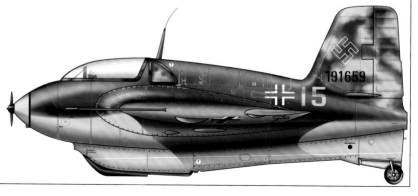

Messerschmitt Me 163B (WNr 191659) from the 6./JG 400. This "yellow 15" was captured at Husum by the British and has been on display since 1976 at the Museum of Flight at East Fortune, Scotland in its original colours and markings. The yellow, visible on the individual number and the front part of the fuselage cone was attributed to the II. Gruppe of the JG 400.

Messerschmitt Me 163B (WNr unknown) from the 1./JG 400, Brandis, November 1944. This Komet was used for the first time in combat by Feldwebel Kurt Schiebeler on 7 August 1944 when he tried unsuccessfully to intercept a Mosquito. The same pilot made other operational sorties, the last in March 1945 (exact date unknown).

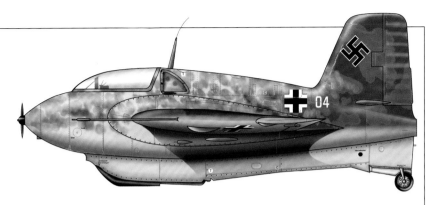

Messerschmitt Me 163B (WNr 191916) from the II./JG 400. Also captured by the English at Husum, this Komet was at first examined at Farnborough in August 1945 in detail, then handed over to Canada the following year. It is now part of Canada's National Aviation Museum collections, where it was entirely restored in 2000.

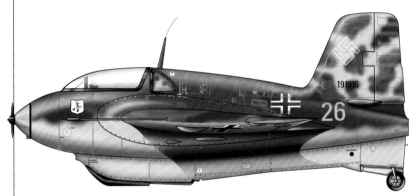

Messerschmitt Me 163B (WNr unknown) from the 14./JG 400, Esperstedt, February 1945. This "white 54" wing roots panels were unpainted, or even left bare metal. Originating with the IV./EJG 2, the III./JG 400 (comprising a Stab and the 13. and 14. Staffeln) was formed in December 1944 and given the task of training Komet pilots. The insignia at the front is that of IV./EJG 2 (IV./JG 400) and shows a plane symbolised by a cross emerging from the clouds with a coloured smoke trail. This plane was captured by the Americans and sent stateside where some of its parts were used to put the example below back into service.

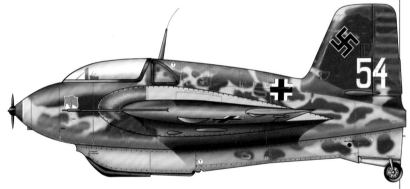

Messerschmitt Me 163B (WNr unknown), from the III./JG 400. Udetfeld, March 1945. Also captured at Husum and recovered by the Americans, this "white 42" (the number on the tailfin was characteristic of training aircraft) was sent to Freeman Field, in the USA in the fall of 1946; there it was given a code, "FE-495" (FE for Foreign Equipment).

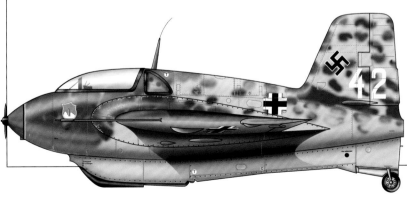

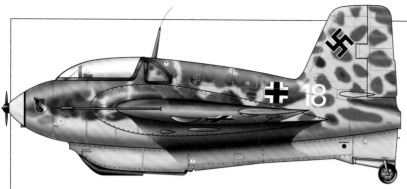

Messerschmitt Me 163B (WNr unknown) from the 1./JG 400, Brandis, August 1944. This Komet was also used by Feldwebel Kurt Schiebeler for an operational sortie in December 1944.

Messerschmitt Me 163 Komet (WNr unknown) from the 13./EJG 2 (13./JG 400). This plane photographed as a wreck after the war has "Schwarze 13" (black 13) on the front, the insignia of the 13./EJG (Ergänzungsgruppe) 2 which became the 13./JG 400 at the end of 1944.

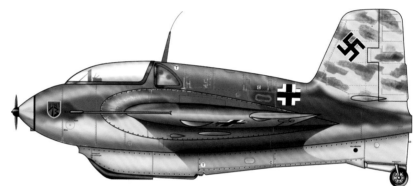

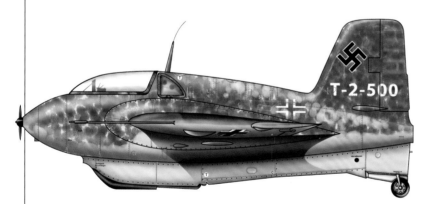

Messerschmitt Me 163 (T-2-500, WNr 191301). Captured by American troops, this Komet was sent stateside and put into service at Muroc Base (now Edwards AFB) in California. There, it only made gliding flights, towed up by a B-29. Because the wood in the wing deteriorated, no powered flight was made in the end so it was then stocked at Norton AFB, California, then sent to Silver Hill in 1954 where it is now on display at the National Air and Space Museum on this base.

Messerschmitt Me 163B (WNr unknown). Captured at Husum by the RAF Regiment, this former "yellow 13" was registered as "Air Ministry 203" which can be seen, painted hastily on the tail; it was sent to Farnborough to be examined and was handed over to France in 1946.

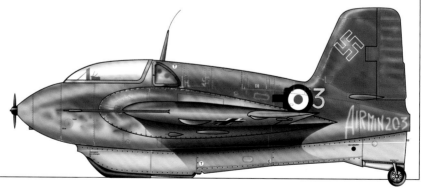

Messerschmitt Me 163B Komet (WNr
310046). Recovered by the British, this plane
was given the serial number "VF 241" and
new roundels, and its intrados was painted
some light colour, generally taken as yellow
(light grey or even white were also possibili-
ties). It was flight-tested by the Royal Aircraft
Establishment (RAE) between 1945 and 1947
as a glider towed by a Spitfire Mk IX, and
was most likely destroyed at the end of these
tests.

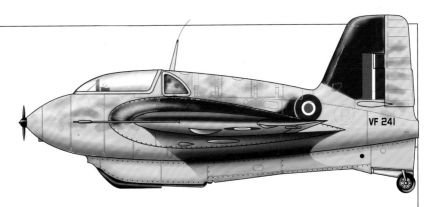

Mitsubishi J8M1 Shusui (sabre blow).
The first two J8M1s flew for the first time,
without any engine, in January 1945, with
the first powered flight taking place only on
7 July. This was just as short as it was tragic
since the plane crashed just after take-
off, killing the pilot, Lieutenant Toyohiko
Inuzuka. No other trial flights took place
before hostilities ceased. Only seven J8M1s
had been completed, whereas not a single
Ki-200 (the version of the fighter intended
for the Imperial Japanese Army Air Force)
had been built.

MXY8 Akigusa (autumn grass). Intended
for training future Sushui pilots, only three
examples of this all-wood glider were built
by the Yokosuka Arsenal, its first flight taking
place on 8 December 1944. Like all Japanese
training aircraft it is painted orange all over.

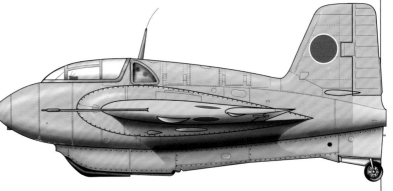

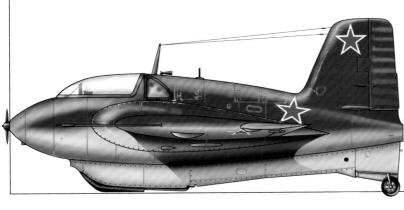

Messerschmitt Me 163 Komet. Captured by the
Soviets, repainted in Soviet colours and with a
new camouflage scheme (dark green on the upper
surfaces, light blue underneath), this example
was tested in the NII VVS (Institute of Aeronautical
Research of the Soviet Air Force) in Moscow, in
particular by the test pilot Vladimir Golofastov in
1945-46. Note the modifications made by the new
owners: radio aerials, Venturi tubes behind the
canopy, etc.

73

HEINKEL HE 162

The Heinkel 162 was created at a time of great difficulties, while German territory was being submitted to almost incessant bombing which disorganised its industrial production and while development of the only machine really capable of countering the Allied bomber formations in any effective manner, the Me 262, was paralysed by Hitler's desire to turn it into a bomber.

Indeed at the end of February 1944, a week of almost uninterrupted Allied air raids almost decapitated German production but this provoked a spectacular recovery from the following summer onwards, mainly because of the particularly energetic measures taken. With this recovery in mind, Albert Speer (at the time the head of the Reichsministerium für Rüstung und Kriegsproduktion, or RMfRuK – Minister of War Production) started on 1 March 1944 by creating the Jägerstab, putting at its head Karl Otto Saur who took charge of Luftwaffe re-equipment. On 1 August 1944, this organisation was discarded and all departments dealing with combat aircraft production in Germany were transferred to the RMfRuK. Absolute priority was given to fighters so as to be able to counter effectively the American and English bombers which were incessantly pounding the country,

the former by day and the latter by night. The Messerschmitt Me 262 turned out to be more complicated to produce than planned (in August 1944, only some 120 examples of the Schwalbe had been produced) because of, among other things, the two-engine configuration and its delicate handling, and the urgent need to have a machine available which was simple to make and to fly; this made the authorities turn almost inevitably to the "Volksjäger" (People's fighter) concept, a decision supported by the fact that a jet's life cycle was, at the time, particularly short, from five to ten missions only.

Supported by Göring himself in this matter, Saur developed the idea of a simply-designed jet fighter, capable of outclassing conventional planes and piloted by members of the Hitler Youth, which itself was a huge breeding ground. Once the raids had been stemmed, the second phase of the plan envisaged building rockets capable of destroying the enemy capitals and thus regaining the initiative.

This programme was totally fanatical from the outset and was considered by many to be unrealistic but it was nonetheless put into operation. On 8 September 1944 a tender was put out for bids from among the main German aircraft builders (Arado, Blohm und Voss, Fieseler, Focke Wulf, Heinkel, Junkers and Messerschmitt) for a fighter which was cheap to build, simply-designed, using nonstrategic materials and needing only semi-skilled or unskilled labour. The machine was built around the BMW 109-003, initially planned for the Me 262 and rated at 1 760 lb s.t. (800 kgp), and armed with two MK 108 30-mm cannon. The specified speed was 470 mph (750 kph), with a range of at least thirty minutes' flight, taking off in less than 545 yards (500 m), weighing a total of two tons. The specifications required the

Top.
"White 23" (WNr 120230), one of three He 162 recovered by the Americans, photographed at Leck just after it was captured by the British. *(USAF)*

Opposite.
The first He 162 (WNr 200001) when it came off the production line at Vienna-Schwechat at the beginning of December 1944, a few days before its maiden flight.

prototype to be ready on 1 December 1944 and for production to start the following month. As he thought the conditions were totally unrealistic, Willy Messerschmitt at once refused to take part in the venture; anyway he was too busy as it was with developing his own Me 262. Three conferences were held on 15, 19 and 30 September after which Heinkel's P.1073 project was preferred to Blohm und Voss' P-211. The P-211 project was a low wing monoplane with a triangular cross-sectioned fuselage with an air intake in the nose, a swept-back tail element placed on the top of a boom, with the engine exhaust nozzle beneath it. Although this project was more than likely the most suitable, except for mass production, it was turned down in the end, a choice which was more of a whim than a well though-out decision…

Things went well and a reduced scale model was presented to General Lucht and several RLM experts at Göring's HQ at Vienna-Schwechat on 23 September, followed five days later by an order for 1 000 machines given to Ernst Heinkel, which for him in a way was revenge after the failures of his He 118, 178 and 280. The problem of pilots had been solved by dipping into the huge breeding ground that was the Hitler Youth and it was decided that in the case of an accident, time wasn't to be wasted repairing damaged aircraft, as they were going to be built in sufficiently large numbers.

An ambitious programme

On 17 October a conference held at the RLM head office organised the future machine's production schedule, a series of 1 000 sets of plans were to be supplied to the various programme participants who were given the job of starting production on 1 November 1944. The planned production rate was for 4 000 machines per month: 1 000 made by Heinkel, in its Marienehe factory (in the Rostock suburbs), 1 000 by Junkers at Bernberg (in Sachse-Anhalt) and 2 000 by Mittelwerke GmbH in Nordhausen, in the underground factories in the Harz Mountains. Junkers made the master copy from which three sets of tooling were to be supplied to the three main sub-contractors.

Production was to increase gradually with 1 000 planes coming off the production lines in April 1945 and 2 000 the following month. As for the BMW engines, they were to be built in the underground factories at a rate of 6 000 per month, of which 2 000 by Mittelwerke alone; these figures were never in fact reached – and by far – because of the circumstances and because of the way the war was going. As for the tooling, there were a lot of delays, Junkers being incapable of supplying it in time and in sufficient quantities because its factories were constantly being bombed. The very last examples were therefore made directly by Heinkel in an underground factory sheltering in a former gypsum mine at Hinterbrühl, near Vienna, a lot of the labour force coming from the concentration camps and especially Matthausen. This forced labour was treated like slaves and forced to work in terrible conditions, in rarefied air and unbearable heat.

"White 23", this time at Wright Field in the United States in 1945, still in its original colours but with the tail fins from WNr 120222. This plane is nowadays part of the collection of the Smithsonian Institute of Washington, DC. (USAF)

TECHNICAL SPECIFICATIONS He 162A-2

Type
Single seat jet fighter

Powerplant
One axial flow BMW 003E-1 turbojet rated at 1 760 lbf (800 kg)

Dimensions
Wingspan: 23 ft 6 in (7.20 m)
Length: 29 ft 7 in (9.05 m)
Wing area: 120.125 sq ft (11.16 m2)
Height: 8 ft 6 in (2.60 m)
Weight (empty): 3 658 lb (1 663 kg)
Max. Weight (loaded): 6 171 lb (2 805 kg)

Performance
Max. Speed: 494 mph (790 kph) at sea level.
525 mph (840 kph) at 19,700 ft (6 000 m)
478 mph (765 kph) at 36,000 ft (11 000 m).

Operating ceiling: 39,200 ft (12 000 m)
Rate of climb: 4 270 ft (1 300 m/min)
Range: 387 mph (620 km) at 19 700 ft (6 000 m); 609 mph (975 km) at 36 000 ft (11 000 m)
Range (max. power): 20 minutes at sea level. 57 minutes at 36 000 ft (11 000 m)

Armament
Two 20-mm Mauser MG 151/20 cannon with 120 rounds (He 162A-2) or two 30 mm MK 108 cannon with 50 rounds (He 162A-0 and A-1).

Two teams of twelve men were entrusted with the project, led by Karl Schwärtzler, the head of research, and Siegfried Günther, the project manager. Officially called the Salamander and Spatz by Heinkel, it was given the designation Heinkel 500 at first; this was then changed to He 162, in order to confuse possible spies by making them believe it was a project that Heinkel had launched a long time ago, a ploy used some years earlier by Messerschmitt for the Me 163.

The new plane's first flight took place at Schwechat (near Vienna), where the machines were assembled, on 6 December 1944, less than three months (89 days to be precise) after the project was launched, which really was an exploit though it can readily be explained by the fact that the team had already been working since the spring on the P.1073 project, a machine powered by an in-house engine, the Heinkel-Hirth HeS 11. With Flugkapitän Gotthold Peter, Heinkel's chief test pilot, at the controls this M1 (WNr 200001) very quickly revealed its longitudinal instability because the engine was positioned on the back of the fuselage and also because the tailfins were too small, two factors penalising lateral stability whilst at the same time causing a tendency to veer to the left. Despite all this, the plane reached 525 mph (840 kph) at 1 900 ft (600 m), but this first flight ended with the plane losing one of its undercarriage doors most likely due to a hinge defect.

The He 162s in JG 1 on the base at Leck, as they were discovered by the British in May 1945. The planes (more than twenty of them) were lined up carefully on either side of the runway, some of them with their engines covered. Note the variety of their decorations.

76

A few days later on 10 December, a real tragedy took place, which in other circumstances would have raised doubts about the whole project. On the same airfield with the same pilot at the controls, the M1 was flying at high speed (about 456 mph—730 kph) in front of an assembly of bigwigs, when suddenly the right-hand wing leading edge broke away, causing the plane to make a series of rapid spins off to the right. The ailerons and the wing tip quickly broke off, followed by the tail and finally the leading edge on the left-hand wing. Completely off balance the plane crashed killing Gotthold Peter. The cause of this dramatic accident were quickly brought to light: a defect in the quality of the alloys used. More mundanely, this demonstration should never have taken place without the M1 undergoing a complete overhaul after its first flight, but official demands and the circumstances at the time decided otherwise.

From prototype to series production

Despite this tragedy, the development pace didn't alter and the second prototype (M2/WNr 200002), identical to the first, flew on 22 December with Karl Francke, the manager of Heinkel, at the controls, with the next two – M3 and M4 – being in turn ready by 16 January 1945. These two machines were in fact different from their predecessors in that their wingtips were pointed downwards at an angle of 55°, the trailing edge of wing nearest the fuselage had been redesigned, the tail (fin and elevators) had been enlarged, the wing structure had been reinforced and ballast had been added above the front undercarriage wheel well to move the centre of gravity forward.

The first batch of 31 machines built were reserved for tests, with the planes taken directly off the production lines and changed into prototypes after being specially modified for the various tests. As for the production series, because of the situation, it was launched before the fighter's first flight. In the emergency and against all the rules, some of the prototypes were transformed into pre-production series machines (He 162A-0), and the last ones – M11 to M36 – became production series aircraft (A-1 and A-2) straight off, with the serial numbers (Werknummern) 220001 to 220024; they were used at the same time for various tests: installing a Jumo 109-004B1 rated at 1 980 lb s.t. thrust (900 kgp) on M11 and M12; as an He162S, an engineless two seat version to be used as a training glider for M16 and M17; combining a jet engine with a BMW 003R rocket engine; or lengthening the fuselage to gain lateral stability. On the M22, the wing leading edges were modified and spoilers installed at the wing root; this disposition was then adopted on the production series planes, the idea being to delay the streams of air stalling at the wingtips.

Because of the conditions prevalent in Germany at the time, it was decided to disperse the fighter's production: the engines to be made at Urseburg, the fuselages at the Heinkel factories at Rostock and Junkers at Bernburg still standing. A host of sub-contractors specialising in woodwork with (e.g. furniture makers) in the Stuttgart and Erfurt areas were also put to work, producing wings, tails, or fuselage noses. This scattering apparently had no effect on the overall quality, mainly because enough copies of the documents were supplied to the various participants and especially because the project had been given top priority (Kurzfristige Lieferplane or short-term delivery programme), the only difficulties encountered being shipping the various finished sections to where they were to be put together. As the Tyrol region had been evacuated in March 1945, most of the production (from WNr 120001 on) had been moved to Marienehe, the main setback being the engines of which not enough were available compared with the number of airframes actually built.

Technical description

The He 162's fuselage was a monocoque design, with sunken rivets mainly made of duralumin. The oval-section nose was made of one-piece plywood, moulded into shape and containing the Pitot tube. The cockpit was protected in the front by 20-mm of armour which also acted as ballast; the rear of the cockpit was also protected by a plate just as thick and the same shape as the main frame. The canopy consisted of a windshield without frames and a removable, jettisonable part opening backwards on two hinges. The pilot got into the cockpit by using a retractable stepladder behind the left cannon deflector. The pilot's bucket seat, designed by Heinkel, was ejected by firing a single cartridge and triggered by pulling on a lever located on the left-hand handle. The instrument panel was itself armoured (8-mm thick) and surmounted by Revi 16 sights; in order to respect

He 162 WNr 120007 ("Yellow 7") on display in 1945 at Wright Field (United States) together with other Luftwaffe planes, including a Ju 290, rechristened "Alles Kaputt"! (USAF)

THE HE 162 PROTOTYPES

Designation Versuchsmuster/ Model	Serial N°/ Registration (Werknummer)	Observations
M1	200001/VI+IA	1st flight 6/12/44, crashed 10/12/44
M2	200002/VI+IB	1st flight 22/12/44, d° M1
M3 — A-1	200003/VI+IC	1st flight 16/1/45, enlarged tail, dipped wing tips, crashed 2/45
M4 — A-1	200004/VI+ID	1st flight 16/1/45, d° M3
M5 — A-1	200005	Never flew, used for ground tests
M6 — A-1	200006/VI+IF	1st flight 23/1/45
M7 — A-2	200007/VI+IG	1st plane armed with 2 MG 151/20
M8 — A-2	200008/VI+IH	1st flight 27/1/45, d° M7, crashed 12/3/45
M9	200009/VI+II	
M10	200010/VI+IJ	
M11 — A-2	220017/WA+??	Jumo 004B engine. Never flew
M12 — A-2	220018/WA+??	Never flew, d° M11.
M13	Not attributed	
M14	Not built (HeS 011 envisaged)	
M15	D° M14	
M16 — A-2	220019	Prototype for He 162S glider
M17 — A-2	220020	D° M16
M18 — A-2	220001/VI+IK	1st flight 24/1/45 1st plane built at Hinterbrühl
M19 — A-2	220002/VI+IL	1st flight 28/1/45. Crash 14/3/45
M20 — A-2	220003/VI+IM	1st flight 10/2/45. Tail tests.
M21 — A-2	220004/VI+IN	Weapons trials, damaged 7/3/45
M22 — A-2	220005/VI+IO	1st flight 22/2/45
M23 — A-2	220006/VI+IP	1st flight 19/3/45
M24 — A-2	220007/VI+IQ	1st flight 20/3/45
M25 — A-2	220008/VI+IR	1st flight 17/2/45. Lengthened fuselage + MK 108 cannon. Destroyed 2/3/45
M26 — A-2	220009/VI+IS	1st flight 17/2/45. D° M25
M27 — A-2	220010/VI+IT	Reserve plane
M28 — A-2	220011/VI+IU	Reserve plane
M29 — A-2	220012/VI+IV	Reserve plane. 1st flight 19/2/45
M30 — A-2	220013/VI+IW	Reserve plane. 1st flight 24/2/45. Weapons trials, EZ 42 gunsight
M31	220014/VI+IX	Reserve plane. Destroyed (bombing)
M32	220015/VI+IY	1st flight 15/3/45. Weapons trials
M33	220016/VI+IZ	1st flight 14/3/45. Weapons trials
M34	220021 (220022?)	
M35	220023	
M36	220024	
M37	220025	
M38	220026	
M39	220027	
M40	220028	
M41	220029	Replaced M25, longer fuselage
M42	220030	

The first 20 machines produced at Hinterbrühl (WNr. 220001 to 220020/A-01 to A-020) were pre-production series examples.

The narrow-tracked (1.66 m) undercarriage had a large wheelbase and for simplicity's sake the main undercarriage legs were borrowed off the Me 109. They retracted hydraulically backwards and lowering the undercarriage was by means of springs which were compressed when the wheels were up; the wheel well door closed or opened by means of a jointed rod linked to the leg.

The wing – trapezoid and one-piece with T-shaped longerons – was made of wood (beech plywood) and had no inspection panels because of its glued skin surface, inspections being carried out with special tools from the outside, once the duralumin wing tips had been removed. The company, Erwin Behr, from Wendlingen am Neckar, whose job it was to find a new process for gluing the wood used a phenol base, called FZ Tego Film to replace the earlier Goldschmitt Tego-Film, a process which was afterwards used on the Me 163 and Me 262. The thickness of the covering was 5 mm on the upper surfaces and 4 mm elsewhere with the join between the fuselage and the engine being completed by a wood or metal fillet.

The wings were fixed to the fuselage by means of four bolts. Its dihedral was small (3°) except for the win tips which pointed sharply downwards at an angle of 55°; the leading edge was straight and the trailing edge was swept forwards. The ailerons and flaps were also made of plywood. An extra 66-gallon (300-litre) tank of fuel was situated in the central part of the wing between the longerons and the inside was covered with a special resin which made it watertight.

The BMW 003E1 (or E2) "Sturm" engine was fixed by means of three bolts to the wing, which meant that maintenance was made much easier. This engine was the same as the ones used by the Arado 234 and had a life of about fifty hours between major services, with the blades having to be checked every ten hours. Lighter but less powerful than the Jumo, it was the only other jet engine to be mass produced during the war; it was rated at 1760 lb s.t. (800 kg) at 9 500 rpm whilst weighing only a little over 1 430 lb (650 kg). Fitted with a seven-stage turbo-compressor, its annular combustion chamber comprised sixteen injectors; its exhaust pipe had a variable surface thanks to the internal cone which an electric motor installed in the external cone moved. Thus the ideal engine rpm was controlled directly from the cockpit to get the optimal temperature. Behind the edge of the engine air intake, whose lower part was actually a radia-

the idea of it being a "people's fighter" the number of instruments was deliberately reduced... Under the instrument panel and between the pilot's legs where the rear part of the front undercarriage well was located, was a small window, a simple way to check whether the landing gear was down or not. Behind the cockpit was the ammunition supply, two 120-round magazines each ending in a duct for feeding the guns. The main fuel tank 143 gallons (650 litres) was located between this compartment and the main undercarriage wheel wells.

The tail section, made of light alloy and with a pronounced dihedral and constant cord, was fitted to the rear of the fuselage, and the twin fins were made of wood with light alloy tips; the two rudders were made of plywood fitted with a fixed Dural tab.

tor, there was 5 ½-gallon (25 litre) oil tank as well as a second tank containing 1 ½ gallons (7 ½ litres) of petrol for the 10 bhp Riedel two-stroke engine used to start the turbojet.

Finally the armament originally consisted of two 30-mm cannon located on either side of the fuselage. These were replaced by two 120-round 20-mm MG 151 cannon because they were lighter, on each of the production series machines (He 162A-1 and A-2s); heavier armament was envisaged (50-round 30-mm MK 108s) for the He 162A-3s but mass production was never started.

Operational training

The first Heinkel 162A-1s and A-2s were built in the underground factory at Hinterbrühl from 20 January 1945 on and sent to Rechlin-Roggentin at once, to the Erprobungskommando 162, the test unit created alongside JG3 and also called the Einsatzkommando Bär, after its CO, the famous Jagdwaffe ace, Heinz Bär. Although at first it had been planned to form a special unit, the JG 80 (January 1945), equipped only with the Volksjäger, this idea was quickly put aside and finally JG 1 "Oesau", flying Fw 190s at the time, was chosen to become the first group to be equipped with the new jet.

The group HQ and its CO, Oberst Herbert Ihlefeld were sent to Lechfeld to get familiar with the machine, then the He 162s made by Heinkel in its Rostock-Marienehe industrial complex were sent to Parchim, about seventy miles to the south on 6 February 1945, to be assigned to the I. Gruppe, commanded by Oberleutnant Emil Demuth, which had transferred its Fw 190s to the II. Gruppe.

On 12 February, thirty or so Spatzes were operational which, in itself, was a sort of exploit, since the official tender had been put out only five months earlier, almost day for day, and the maiden flight of the first prototype had taken place only two months before. On 24 February, 2./JG 1 was sent to Vienna-Heidfeld to

convert to the Spatz whilst the 3. Staffel was transferred to Parchim for the same reason.

II/JG 1, commanded by Paul Heinrich Dahne, started converting from the Fw 190 to the He 162 and settled at Warnemünde on 7 April. The last unit of the Group, III/JG 1, was in turn withdrawn from the front in March 1945 for conversion but in the end never received any machines. Disbanded on 24 April, its personnel was used to reinforce other units [1].

A few days on the front

After a quick conversion plagued by crashes caused by a variety of breakdowns (fuel supply, etc.), especially engine fires, and with the Vienna factory and its airfield having to be evacuated in the face of the oncoming Russian troops, the whole of I./JG 1 was assembled at Parchim which it had to leave anyway on 9 April after the base's installations were put out of action by a massive USAAF air raid two days earlier. Transiting via Ludwigslust, where it was joined by the Stab, it finally settled at Leck (in Holstein, near the Danish border) on 15 April where II./JG 1 – without any machines – joined it on the 30th.

A few days after the end of the fighting, on 4 May, all the groups were assembled in the I (Einsatz) and the II. (Sammel)/JG 1 [2].

I./JG 1 was declared operational at Leck on 15 April 1945, but its effectiveness was constantly hampered by the recurrent lack of fuel. Moreover when they were able to fly, the He 162s had a lot of accidents, mainly because of their very short range – only half an hour – which forced the pilots to look for an emergency

Because of its particularly short operational career, shots of the He 162 in flight are very rare. Here is one of the few known ones of a JG 1 Spatz landing, with flaps and undercarriage down.

Above.
Still at Leck, Oberleutnant Demuth, "Staka" (Staffelkapitän) of 3./JG 1 posing in front of his He 162 "Yellow 11".

Above, right.
Another shot of the pilots of JG 1. The Spatz behind them ("White 6" from 1./JG 1) has a partly camouflaged fuselage, leaving the undercoat covering the joints on the skin.

landing ground with the engine out of fuel, or even to eject. Worse, and totally contradicting the thinking which had led to its creation, the Spatz remained a little horror to fly, a plane that only a few veterans were actually capable of mastering, and not novices straight out of the Hitler Youth with only a few hours gliding to their credit… The Spatz's "stubborn" character caused the death of several test pilots after the war, like Flight Lieutenant Marcks who was killed aboard one of them during trials carried out at Farnborough, or

VERSIONS AND VARIANTS

– Versions produced

He 162A-0: Pre-production series. 10 examples built.

He 162A-1: Production series, two 30-mm MK 108 cannon, abandoned in favour of the A-2.

He 162A-2: Main production series version, two 20 mm MG 151 cannon.

– Planned versions, not produced

He 162A-3: Improved version, two 30-mm MK 108 cannon

He 162A-8: Jumo 004D-4 jet engine.

He 162A-9: Variant of the A-2 with butterfly tail.

He 162B-1: Heinkel-Hirth HeS 011A jet engine rated at 2 860 lb s.t. (1 300 kgp), longer fuselage containing more fuel to increase range; increased wingspan but reduced dihedral in order to suppress the dipped wing tips; two 30-mm MK 108 cannon; airframe could also be powered by two Argus As 044 pulse-jets.

He 162C-1: Fuselage of the He 162B, Heinkel-Hirth HeS 011A jet engine, swept wing (15°) without dihedral, butterfly tail, two 30-mm MK 108 cannon fitted obliquely behind the cockpit in the Schräge Musik configuration.

He 162D-1: like the He 162C, but with forward swept wings.

He 162E: He 162A with mixed powerplants: BMW 003R (BMW 003A turbojet incorporating a liquid fuel BMW 718 rocket engine installed just above the exhaust nozzle of the turbojet in order to increase thrust). One prototype was built and perhaps flight-tested.

He 162S: Two-seat training glider.

Captain Schlienger, who suffered the same fate at the CEV at Mont-de-Marsan (France) in July 1948.

Because Allied fighters were all over German territory, it wasn't long before they encountered some He 162s. On 15 April, a pilot from I./JG 1 who was on his fourth training flight was faced with some Spitfires, but refused to fight. Four days later, a Tempest pilot from N° 222 Squadron, Fl. Off. Geoff Walkington, out strafing the airfield at Husum, declared shooting down an "unknown type of plane, with green speckled camouflage and a yellow belly (sic), with twin tail and a single engine. The nose of the plane seemed to droop and the wings seen from above resembled an Me 109's." The plane claimed by Walkington was most likely one of the two He 162s officially declared lost in combat. It was piloted by Feldwebel Günther Kirchner and was shot down shortly after taking off, trying to intercept enemy bombers with other jets. The second official loss took place on 26 (or 25, depending on the sources) April when Uffz Rechenbach crashed after shooting down an English plane.

As for the He 162's tally during its very brief operational career, things are even more complicated because the kills claimed cannot be confirmed by any accounts that agree, though nowadays two kills are generally accepted. As mentioned above, the first was scored on 25 (or 26) April during I./JG 1's first operational sortie against a RAF Mosquito raid, and the second took place on 4 May when Leutnant Rudolf Schmitt declared having shot down a Typhoon [3].

On 5 May 1945, Admiral Hans-Georg von Freiderburg ordered German troops in Northwest Europe (NW Germany, Holland and Denmark) to surrender and JG 1 was therefore grounded. When British troops of the 11th Armoured Division (the "Bulls") reached Leck on 15 May [4], thirty or so He 162s [5]

---

1. Certain sources mention that it was envisaged to equip the I. and II./JG 400 with He 162s because the Me 163, with which they were equipped, did not have along enough range.
2. The Einsatzgruppe I./JG 1 gathered together the operational pilots and II., the rest of the personnel, mainly non-flying personnel and ground crews.
3. A Tempest is sometimes mentioned though in some texts this kill is attributed to a flak battery.
4. There is some doubt as to the exact date that the airfield was invested, 16 May also being a possible date. On the other hand, 8 May, often mentioned and which corresponds to the armistice in Europe, is not possible because this day the British were still around of Hamburg.
5. According to the British sources, the Allies captured 31 He 162 on the whole German territory, Austria (annexed to the time) included, of which 27 only at Leck.

Above.
He 162A-2 (WNr 120086) from 2./JG 1 was one of the Salamanders recovered by the British. Renamed "Air Ministry N° 62", it was put on display at Hyde Park in London in September 1945 and finally sent to Canada. It is nowadays part of the Canadian Aviation Museum collections.

were lined up on either side of Leck airfield's main strip. At the end of its few weeks' activity, JG 1, the only Luftwaffe unit equipped with the Heinkel plane had lost ten pilots and 13 machines, only two of which in combat.

At the time of the Armistice, 120 (116?) He 162s had been delivered, about 200 others had been finished and several hundred others (600?) were found at different stages of completion. The definitive version of the fighter, whose mass production was planned, was to have been powered by an HeS 11 rated at 2 860 lb s.t. (1 300 kgp) and equipped with a butterfly tail, a configuration already tried out on the Heinkel 280. When hostilities ceased, the plane's prototype was only half finished and was captured by the Allies. The Spatz's career continued after the war since the Allies shared out the thirty or so examples that were fit for flying. Ten of them were quickly destroyed where they were, but the British held on to ten others of which at least three were flight-tested. Of the three He

162s which were given to the USA, two were flight-tested and the third was completely dismantled so it could be studied. France was given five of them (two A-1s and three A-2s) which were studied in the spring of 1946 at the SNCAC, where it was decided that only the A-2s would be made airworthy with the first trials taking place in April and May 1947 at Orléans-Bricy, then at the CEAM at Mont-de-Marsan. There they continued until 23 July 1948 when a test pilot was killed aboard one of the machines (WNr 120223). The Soviets managed to get two He 162A-2s flying at the Rostock factory and tried them out in May 1946 at the Institute for Aeronautical Research at Zhukovsky, before sending them to the Moscow TsAGI (Central Institute for Aero-hydrodynamics) to be studied.

As a matter of fact, there was a project for licence building the Spatz in Japan which followed on from a delegation of Japanese officials visiting the Heinkel factory at Rostock in April 1945. Here again events decided otherwise… ❑

Above.
One of the five He 162s recovered by France, the N°2, formerly "Yellow 21" from I./JG 1. This plane was completely repainted light grey, with tricolour roundels and flashes.

Opposite.
This "Red 02" was one of the two He 162s tried out by the Soviets at the Remensk LII at the end of 1945. Repainted light grey (or aluminium) it bears red stars on the fuselage and tails.

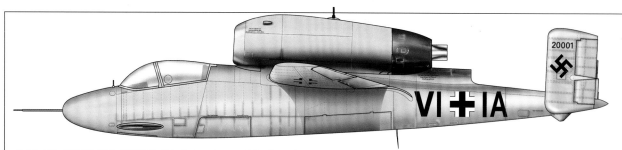

Heinkel He 162 M1 (WNr 200001). This first prototype of the Spatz (sparrow, the fighter's official name) made its first flight on 6 December 1944 at Vienna-Schwechat and crashed there four days later (10 December) during a demonstration flight in front of the Luftwaffe general staff, Heinkel-Süd's test pilot, Flugkapitän Gotthold Peter, killing himself in the accident.

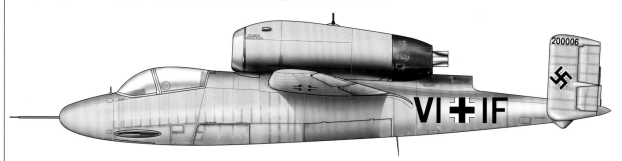

Heinkel He 162 M6 (WNr 200006). This prototype, which made its first flight on 23 January 1945, was mainly intended for MK 108 canon trials on the A-1 version. The prototypes and the pre-production series machines were all painted the same colour, no doubt RLM 76 grey, as shown here although other sources indicate RLM 02 greenish grey.

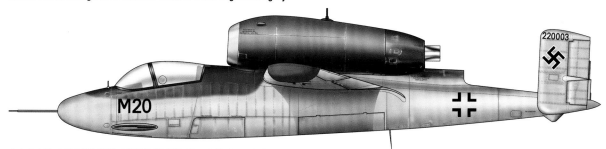

Heinkel He 162 M20 (WNr 220003/VI+IM). Specially intended for simplified undercarriage trials, this pre-production series machine made its first flight on 10 February 1945 and crashed two weeks later. Its wreck is visible on several shots just before the armistice on the airfield at Munich-Riem, together with the M23. The fact that these machines were present on this base at the same time as JV 44 which also used it, suggests that this unit might also have been given Spatzes as well as its Me 262s.

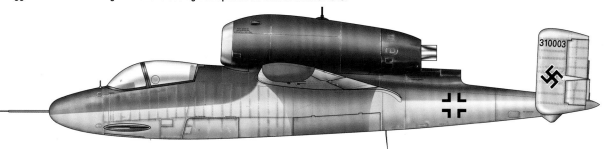

Heinkel He 162A-1 (WNr 310003) built by Dora Mittelwerke in Nordhausen and never assigned to a unit. Its camouflage is unusual, with the fuselage and the engine being painted RLM 82 or 83 green instead of the regulation RLM 81.

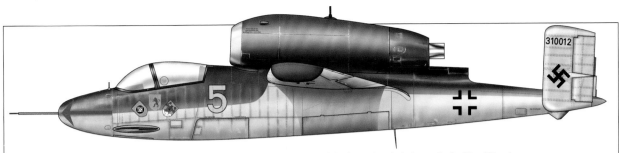

Heinkel He 162A-1 (WNr 310012) from the 3./JG 1. Recovered by the French in the end and photographed without its wings, on a wagon, this plane has three insignia under the canopy corresponding, in order: to the JG 1 since the end of 1943 (a winged 1), to the 3./JG 1 (red lion rampant, in fact the arms of the town of Dantzig) and to the I./JG 1 (a devil emerging from a cloud).

Heinkel He 162A-1 (WNr 310018) in the 1./JG 1, Leck, May 1945. This "White 5" belonged to Hauptmann Heinz Künnecke, 1./JG 1's Staffel-kapitän. The camouflage scheme is typical of Junkers-built machines, with the colour of the upper fuselage (RLM 81 Braunviolett) curving upwards at the wing roots.

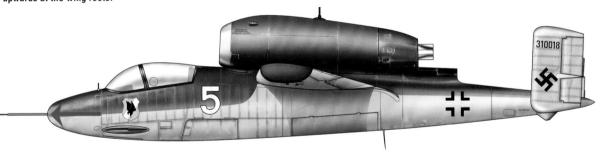

Heinkel He 162A-2 (WNr 120017) from the Stab of the JG 1, Ludwiglust, April 1945. At Leck, three machines photographed after they had been captured had their fuselages painted with three colours (black, white and red), perhaps indicating that they belonged to the Geschwa-dersstab.

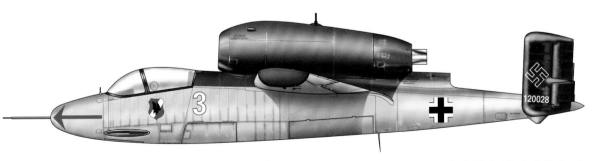

Heinkel He 162A-2 (WNr 120028) from the 1./JG 1, Leck, May 1945. The production series machines built by Heinkel at Rostock-Marienehe had a serial number (here painted at the bottom of the tail fins) starting with 1200xx.

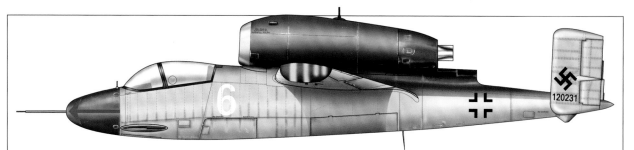

Heinkel He 162A-2 (WNr 120231) from the 1./JG 1, Leck, May 1945. Apart from its dark coloured cone (RLM 81, as shown here) and its original scheme on the wing tips, this "White 6" front fuselage section was left unpainted.

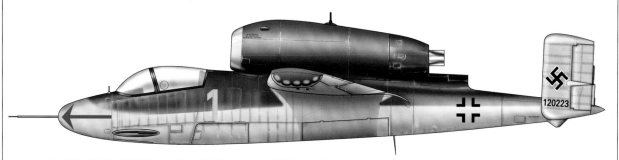

Heinkel He 162A-2 (WNr 120023) from the 3./JG 1, Leck, May 1945. Note the special painting of the wing tips, RLM 76 light grey, making circular patches on the RLM 81 of the upper surfaces. The right hand tailfin from this machine was fitted to the He 162 now on display at the Musée de l'Air et de l'Espace at Paris-Le Bourget.

Heinkel He 162A-2 (WNr uncertain: 120013 or 120027) from the 1./JG 1, Leck, 4 May 1945. Leutnant Rudolf Schmitt declared that he had shot down a Hawker Typhoon (or a Tempest…) on 4 May 1945 aboard this plane. This kill was not confirmed by anybody or by any official document and would, if true, be the only one obtained by the "Volksjäger" during its very brief operational career. Note the black and white fuselage cross, rather unusual at the time.

Heinkel He 162A-2 (WNr 120027) from the 1./JG 1, Ludwiglust, April 1945. Pilot: Leutnant Rudolf Schmitt, Staffelkapitän. Even today, the exact meaning of the red arrow painted on the front of the Spatzes in JG 1 is uncertain; this decoration was found on a great number of the unit's planes photographed at Leck, when the airfield was captured by the Allies.

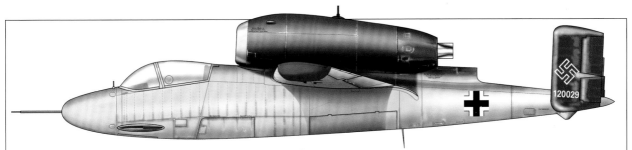

Heinkel He 162A-2 (WNr 120029) without any code or unit insignia.

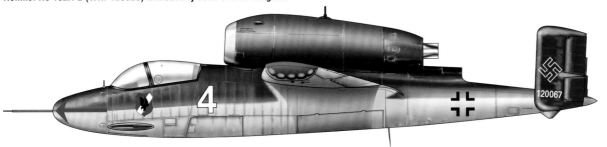

Heinkel He 162A-2 (WNr 120067) from 1./JG 1, Leck, May 1945. This plane was one of those recovered by the Americans and sent stateside.

Heinkel He 162A-2 (WNr 120074) from the 3./JG 1, Leck, May 1945, belonging to 3./JG 1's "Staka" (Staffelkapitän/ Staffel CO), Oberleutnant Emil Demuth. This Spatz has an unusual individual number, the little "Yellow 20" (the Staffel's colour) in fact adopting the I./JG 1's current practice (of which Demuth was one of the Gruppenkommandeure) in which this figure replaced the usual double chevron of his rank. The pilot didn't score the 16 kills aboard this plane but earlier with an Fw 190, the insignia under the canopy being Demuth's former group (I./JG 1). Captured by the British, this He 162 was given the code "Air Min 60".

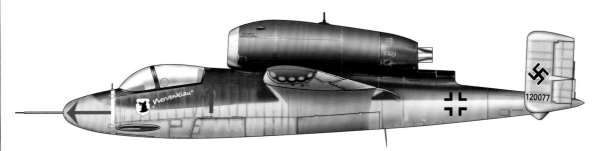

Heinkel He 162A-2 (WNr 120077) from the 2./JG 1, Ludwiglust, April 1945. Built by the factory at Rostock-Marienehe, this plane was usually used by Leutnant Gerhard Harf and on either side of the fuselage bears the insignia of the III./JG 77, the pilot's old unit. The nickname, "Nervenklau" (pain in the neck) recalls Harf's unpleasant habit of riding round the airfield on his motorbike... We have shown here the air intake left unpainted whereas some sources say it was red, the Staffel's colour. This Spatz is nowadays part of the Planes of Fame Museum Collection at Chino, USA.

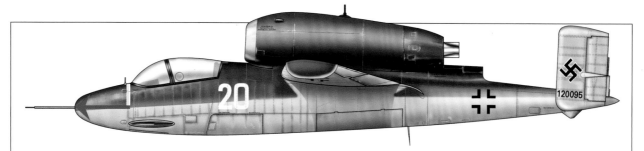

Heinkel He 162A-2 (WNr 120095) from the 1./JG 1 (or the Stab of the JG 1), Leck, May 1945. The reason for the white stripe painted in front of the windshield, also seen on other machines, is unknown.

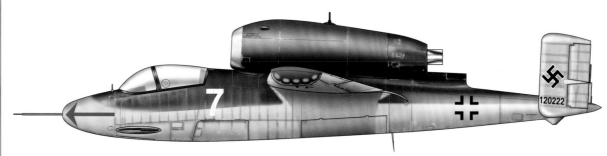

Heinkel He 162A-2 (WNr 120222) from the 1./JG 1. Leck, May 1945.

Heinkel He 162A-2 (WNr 120230) from the Stab of the JG 1, Leck, May 1945. This machine is generally attributed to Oberstleutnant Herbert Ihlefeld, and was one of the three sent stateside for evaluation after the war. Reequipped at Freeman Field with WNr 120222's tails, it is now on display in the National Air & Space Museum, Washington, DC.

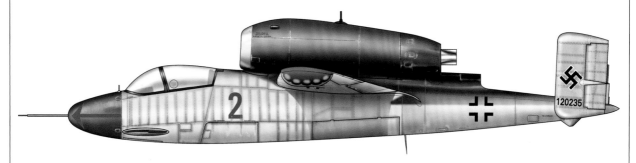

Heinkel He 162A-2 (WNr 120235) from 2./JG 1, Leck, May 1945. The front part of its fuselage was unpainted and only the panel joins were covered with yellowish primer; this Spatz is one of two photographed at Leck after the base was captured and whose fuselage front has been painted a dark colour like RLM 81, as we have shown here, or RLM 82.

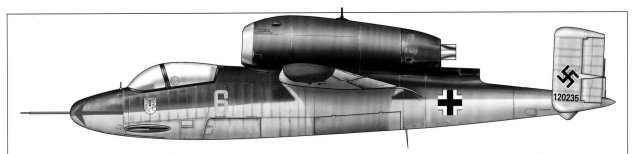

Heinkel He 162A-2 (WNr, possibly, 120235) from the 3./JG 1, Leck, May 1945. It is possible that this machine is the one that is now on display at the Imperial War Museum, London. Each Staffel in the JG 1 had a distinctive colour, used especially for the individual numbers: white for the 1., red for the 2., and yellow for the 3.

Heinkel He 162A-2 (WNr unkown) from the 1./JG 1, Leck, May 1945. This plane is perhaps the former "22 red", the new individual number having been painted over the old one.

Heinkel He 162A-2 (WNr 120072). This former "3 white" from the 1./JG 1, captured by the English at Leck has had its original markings (cross, insignia and individual number), apart from the red arrow on the nose, painted over and replaced by the new owner's markings. Designated "Air Ministry 61", this plane crashed at Aldershot during a test flight on 9 November 1945.

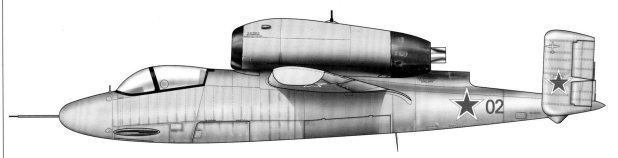

Heinkel He 162A-2 (WNr unknown). This is one of the two He 162s tried out by the Soviets at the LII in Remensk after the end of 1945. The plane had been painted entirely light grey (or aluminium – the poor quality of the few existing photos does not enable the colour to identified) with red stars painted on the fuselage and the fins as well as an individual number, also red.

Arado Ar 234 camouflage

— The prototypes were painted with RLM 70 and 71 with large square angle patches on the upper surfaces, with the underneath painted light blue (Hellblau) RLM 65. The separation between the two was very low down on the fuselage sides. It is possible that these prototypes were painted with a mix of these hues with the new colours: RLM 70 and 82 or RLM 71 and 81.
— The production series machines were painted RLM 81 and 82 on the upper surfaces, and RLM 76 underneath.
(Drawing 1/72)

The Heinkel
162 serial numbers

M1 to M10 : prototypes built by Heinkel at Vienna-Schwechart
120000 + : production series built by Heinkel at Rostock-Marienehe
300000 + :production series built by Junkers at Bernburg.

Heinkel He 162 factory camouflage

The camouflage scheme introduced in January 1945 for the He 162s abandoned the grill system and therefore the sharp-angled patches used previously by the Luftwaffe, and prescribed uniform painting, using the same colour for whole elements of the plane (wings, stabiliser, etc.).
Upper surface of the fuselage, left wing and left horizontal stabiliser: RLM 81.
Wing and right tailplane uppersurfaces + entire reactor : RLM 82.
Fuselage sides, undersides and tailfins : RLM 76

Drawing 1/72 scale

Drawing 1/72 scale

Messerschmitt
163 Serial Numbers

— Me 163A V4 to V13 (WNr 1630000001 to -10): Built by Messerschmitt at Augsburg.
— Me 163B V1 to V69 (WNr 16310010 - 10078): Ditto.
— Me 163B-0 (WNr 440001 - 440020 and 440165 - 44019): Built by Klemm at Böblingen
— Me 163B (WNr 190571 - 190579 and 191090 - 191101, and 191102 - 191124): Built by Junkers at Antonienhof

Messerschmitt 163
camouflage

The prototypes and the first examples of the Me 163 were painted RLM 76 light grey all over. The planes built subsequently were given a camouflage scheme with a base of three shades of grey: RLM 74 and 75 on the upper surfaces and RLM 76 underneath. Most of the production series aircraft used the classic Luftwaffe camouflage scheme introduced in September 1944, consisting of violet-brown RLM 81 and dark green RLM 82 on the upper surfaces with the lower surfaces still painted with light grey RLM 76. According to a directive issued during the last months of the war, the lower surfaces ought not to have been painted at all to save on paint, a measure which was applicable to the Me 163 as its wings were made of wood. Some sources indicate that the machines put into service before the introduction of the new tints should have been painted RML 70 and 71.
Various variations of this general scheme can be seen on the period photos: light grey speckled tail; speckled tail and fuselage front; tail with large patches; fuselage entirely speckled (RLM 81 and 82, grey RLM 74 and 75 were also possible). The Klemm-built Me 163s' fuselages were very densely speckled.

Drawing 1/72 scale

GLOSSARY AND ABBREVIATIONS

Auflärungsgruppe (Aufkl.Gr): Reconnaissance Group
Einsatzkommando (EKdo): Special detachment
Ergänzungsjagdgruppe (EJG): Reserve/replacement fighter group.
Erprobungskommando (EKdo): Operational trials and evaluation detachment.
Erprobungstelle (E.Stelle): Test/evaluation centre
Fernaufklärungsgruppe (FAGr): Long-range reconnaissance group
Feldwebel (Fw): Adjudant.
Flugabwehrkanone (Flak): Anti-aircraft guns (AA)
Gefreiter (Gefr): Corporal.
Geschwader: Squadron, 3 to 4 Gruppen.
Geschwaderstab: Squadron headquarters.
Gruppe (Gr): Group, 3 to 4 Staffeln, e.g. I./JG 26 = 1st Gruppe of Jagdgeschwader 26.
ISS: Industrieschutzstaffel: factory protection squadron

KG: Kampfgeschwader: Bomber squadron (108 - 144 planes).
Jagdwaffe: German equivalent of Fighter Command.
Hauptmann (Hptm): Captain.
JG: Jagdgeschwader: Fighter squadron, 80 to 125 planes
Jabo: Jagdbomber (Fighter bomber)
JV: Jagdverband (Fighter unit)
KG(J): Kampfgeschwader (Jagd): Bomber squadron transformed into a fighter unit
KGr: Kampfgruppe (Bomber group)
Kommandeur (Kdr): Gruppe CO.
Kommodore (Kdre): Squadron CO.
Leutnant (Lt): Lieutenant
Luftflotte: Air fleet, group of squadrons with a responsibility for a zone of operations.
Major (Maj): Major
NAGr: Nahaufklärungsgruppe (Tactical short range recce group)

NJG: Nachtjagdgruppe (Nightfighter group)
Oberfeldwebel (Ofw): Adjudant.
Oberfähnrich (Ofhr): Ensign.
Obergefreiter (Ogfr): Corporal.
Oberleutnant (Oblt): First-lieutenant
Oberst (Obst): Colonel.
Oberstleutnant (Obslt): Lieutenant-colonel
OKL: Oberkommando der Luftwaffe (Luftwaffe general staff)
RLM: Reichsluftfahrtministerium (Air Ministry)
Schwarm: Patrol (4 planes)
Staffel (St ou Sta): Flight (12 planes)
Stab: Unit HQ.
3./JG 7 = 3rd Staffel of the Jagdgeschwader 7
Staka: Staffelkapitän (Staffel CO)
Unteroffizier (Uffz): Sub-lieutenant
Versuchs: Prototype
WNr: Werknummer (Serial number)

Jet aircraft in front line Luftwaffe units as at 9 April 1945

On that day the Luftwaffe had 3 330 combat aircraft at its disposal but barely 200 jets. The Me 262 was by far the most used jet aircraft.

Unit	Planes	Delivered	Available
Stab./JG 7	Me 262	5	4
III./JG 7	Me 262	41	26
I./JG 7	Me 262	30	23
10./NJG 11	Me 262	9	7
I./KG(J) 54	Me 262	7	21
JV 44	Me 262	30	15
Kdo Bonow	Ar 234	2	1
NAGr.6	Me 262	7	3
FAGr 33	Ar 234/Ju 188	13	8
I./KG 51	Me 262	15	11
II./KG 51	Me 262	6	12
Stab./KG 76	Ar 234	2	1
II./KG 76	Ar 234	5	1
III./KG 76	Ar 234	5	1
FAGr.100	Ar 234	6	1
FAGr.123	Ar 234/Ju 188	12	7
Kdo Sommer	Ar 234	3	2

Table made by Vinvent Gréciet in WingMasters Special Issue N°9

THE GERMAN JET AIRCRAFT ACES

Name	Rank	Score	Unit	Total kills (jet) WWII
Welter Kurt	Olt	20+	Kdo Welter, 10./NJG 11	63
Bär Heinrich	Obslt	16	EJG 2, JV 44	220
Schall Franz	Hptm	14	JG 7	137
Buchner Hermann	Ofw	12	Kdo Nowotny, JG 7	58
Eder Georg-Peter	Maj	12	Kdo Nowotny, JG 7	78
Rudorffer Erich	Maj	12	JG 7	222
Schnörrer Karl	Lt	11	EKdo 262, Kdo Nowotny, JG 7	46
Buttner Erich	Ofw	8	EKdo 262, Kdo Nowotny, JG 7	8
Lennartz Helmut	Fw	8	EKdo 262, Kdo Nowotny, JG 7	13
Rademacher Rudolf	Lt	8	JG 7	126
Schuck Walter	Olt	8	JG 7	206
Wegmann Gunther	Olt	8	EKdo 262, JG 7	14
Weihs Hans-Dieter	Lt	8	JG 7	8
Weissenberger Theodor	Maj	8	JG 7	208
Ambs Alfred	Lt	7	JG 7	7
Arnold Heinz	Ofw	7	JG 7	49
Becker Karl-Heinz	Fw	7	10./NJG 11	7
Galland Adolf	GLt	7	JV 44	104
Köster Franz	Uffz	7	EJG 2, JG 7, JV 44	7
Muller Fritz	Lt	6	JG 7	22
Steinhoff Johannes	Obst	6	JG 7, JV 44	176
Baudach Helmut	Ofw	5	Kdo Nowotny, JG 7	20
Ehrler Heinrich	Maj	5	JG 7	206
Grunberg Hans	Olt	5	JG 7, JV 44	82
Heim Joseph	Gfr	5	JG 7	5
Neumann Klaus	Lt	5	JG 7, JV 44	37
Schreiber Alfred	Lt	5	Kdo Nowotny, JG 7	5
Späte Wolfgang	Maj	5	JG 400, JV 44	99

Design and lay-out by Magali Masselin.
Histoire & Collections 2012

ISBN: 978-2-35250-224-1

Publisher's number: 35250

Edited by
HISTOIRE & COLLECTIONS
SA au capital de 182 938, 82 €
5, avenue de la République F-75541 Paris Cedex 11
Tel: +33-1 40 21 18 20
Fax: +33-1 47 00 51 11
www.histoireetcollections.com

This book has been designed, typed, laid-out and processed by Histoire & Collections on fully integrated computer equipment.

Color separation: Studio A & C

Printed by
Calidad Graphicas, Espagne,
November 2012